Five
Life Stories

James W. Fowler
& Robin W. Lovin

with
Katherine Ann Herzog
Brian Mahan
Linell Cady
Jonathan P. Gosser

Abingdon / Nashville

TRAJECTORIES IN FAITH: FIVE LIFE STORIES

Copyright © 1980 by Abingdon

Library of Congress Cataloging in Publication Data

FOWLER, JAMES W   1940-
  Trajectories in faith.
  Bibliography: p.
  1.   Religions—Biography.   2.   Faith—Psychology—Case
studies.   I.   Lovin, Robin W., joint author.   II.   Title.
  BL72.F65   291'.4'2 [B]   79-20485

ISBN 0-687-42480-1

Material from *Letters and Papers from Prison* by Dietrich Bonhoeffer is
reprinted with permission of Macmillan Publishing Co. Inc. From the
Enlarged Edition. Copyright © 1953, 1967, 1971 by SCM Press, Ltd.

Quotations from *Autobiography of Malcolm X* by Malcolm X with the
assistance of Alex Haley, Copyright © 1964 by Alex Haley and Malcolm
X, Copyright © 1965 by Alex Haley and Betty Shabazz. Reprinted by
permission of Random House, Inc.

**MANUFACTURED BY THE PARTHENON PRESS AT
NASHVILLE, TENNESSEE, UNITED STATES OF AMERICA**

Acknowledgments

We take pleasure in acknowledging our gratitude for the key contributions that the following persons made to the preparation of this book.

Funding for editorial and typing assistance came from a grant to the Research Project on Faith and Moral Development from the Joseph P. Kennedy, Jr., Foundation of Washington, D.C. Mrs. Eunice Kennedy Shriver has taken a special interest in this larger research project. Mr. Sargent Shriver made the suggestion that led us to begin biographical examinations of the faith stories of "world transformers."

The members of the seminar at Harvard Divinity School in which these studies originated gave helpful evaluations of them at an early stage.

Our coauthors maintained good humor as we pushed one another through the process of triple revisions and rewrites.

Mr. Roger Ard, doctoral candidate in Christian ethics at Emory University, and research assistant in faith development, deserves special recognition. Roger revised the entire manuscript with an editorial skill and thoroughness that makes this truly his book, too.

The Rev. Fairey Caroland typed the manuscripts with speed and precision. Mr. Jon Caswell, research assistant in faith development, gave the manuscript a careful final reading, making many valuable improvements and corrections.

We hope our readers will share some of the excitement and joy in learning that we have experienced in our work on this volume.

JWF/RWL

Contents

Introduction

Telling the stories of saints and heroes is a universal feature of religious life. Insights into the personality of a great teacher and a narrative that gives the full context of the teaching lend a note of authenticity to the records of instruction. Sometimes the details merely form a setting for the teaching, as in the stories of the Chinese sages that begin: "Chuang Tzu and Hui Tzu were crossing the River Hao near the dam. . . . " Sometimes the events themselves provide an eloquent testimony of faith, as in the heroism of the Maccabees or the sufferings of John Foxe's martyrs. Always, however, the biographical details remind us that saints and heroes are real people whose teachings we repeat and whose lives we honor. Their stories provide glimpses of personal integrity, or inner peace and wisdom, or commitment to a cause. Their stories invite us to enter the structures of faith that supported their lives.

The five biographies that make up this volume explore the structures of faith in the lives of Malcom X, Anne Hutchinson, Blaise Pascal, Ludwig Wittgenstein, and Dietrich Bonhoeffer. Each of their stories, in large measure, speaks for itself, but the studies are guided by a theory of faith development that identifies some common features in the way faith takes shape in different centuries and in very different lives. In this introduction we shall explain the fundamentals of this developmental theory and outline the ways that it guided our writing of the biographies. Before we identify what is new and unique in these stories, however, we need to understand how they are linked to the legends of saints and heroes that all religions tell, and also to the modern, critical forms of religious biography that many of our readers already know well. Each age describes its saints and heroes with its own methods, to meet its own concerns.

From Legend to Biography

Christians in the Middle Ages told life stories that often were shaped more by the need for inspiration than by a need for accuracy. The few eyewitness accounts of Christian martyrs in the early centuries which were preserved from court records or letters written on the spot were expanded over and again by imaginative stories that filled a need for biographical detail even when the facts were not available. The *Golden Legend* of James of Voragine enjoyed a wide circulation even before the invention of the printing press. This collection of facts, traditions, and miracle stories about the saints was designed to inspire popular devotion. Here we read about the ox and the lamb that gave homage to the infant Christ, and about the martyrdom of St. Denis, beheaded on Montmartre, who rose from the block and carried his own head two miles to the village "where he lies to this day, by his own choice and by divine providence."[1]

An immense variety of these "Lives of the Saints" emerged to fill the needs of popular piety and to enrich the observances of the church calendar. Moreover, such stories sometimes served the more parochial interests of a city, church, or shrine that wished to establish an apostolic connection or some sacred past for itself. The impact of this literature on individual lives was sometimes very great. It was just such stories, for example, that Ignatius of

Loyola read during the convalescence that converted him from a chivalric soldier into the ardent Christian who later founded the Jesuit order. The tales themselves, however, were stylized, unhistorical, and, to a modern reader, shallow in characterization and lacking in life.

It remained for Renaissance writers, influenced by the classical histories of Tacitus, Plutarch, and Suetonius, to introduce character and personal detail into the lives of saints and religious heroes. The first subjects of this new biographical realism were secular leaders—or very worldly ecclesiastics. Thomas More wrote a biography of Richard III in 1513, and George Cavendish published his *Life and Death of Cardinal Wolsey* in 1558. More himself became the subject of a more explicitly religious biography, *The Mirrour of Vertue in Worldly Greatness, or the Life of Syr Thomas More*. It was written by his son-in-law, William Roper, and published in 1553. The *Mirrour of Vertue* uses personal details and anecdotes chiefly to stress More's faith and integrity, rather than to exploit the themes of his wealth and power. Roper describes More's departure from his home in Chelsea to face his trial at Lambeth Palace:

> And whereas he evermore used before at his departure from his wife and children whom he tenderly loved, to have them bring him to his boat, and there to kiss them all and bid them farewell; then would he suffer none of them forth of the gate to follow him, but pulled the wicket after him and shut them all from him. And with an heavy heart, as by his countenance it appeared, with me and our four servants there took he his boat towards Lambeth. Wherein sitting still sadly a while, at last he suddenly rounded me in the ear and said: "Son Roper, I thank our Lord the field is won." What he meant thereby I then wist not, yet loath to seem ignorant, I answer: "Sir, I am thereof very glad." But as I conjectured afterwards, it was for that the love he had to God wrought in him so effectually that it conquered all his carnal affections utterly.[2]

11

The appearance of these Tudor period "lives," classical in inspiration but very direct and personal in style, marks the beginning of modern religious biography. Although stories of saints and heroes as expressions of faith are found throughout history, telling the story of a person's faith with attention to individual details and a concern for historical accuracy is a comparatively recent phenomenon, western in its origins.

This new style of religious biography clearly represents an attempt at critical history, rather than a simple expression of piety. Facts count, and the inspirational power of the events must be matched by the quality of the documentation. Even polemical pieces and studies designed for popular devotional use embody this trend toward historical detail. John Foxe's *Book of Martyrs* (1563) is a record of the final acts of Christian martyrs, primarily of Protestants condemned in England during the Catholic restoration under Queen Mary. "As to my book," Foxe wrote in the preface, "I make it known to all that I have taken pains to put in nothing that is fabulous or in any way like their golden (say rather leaden) legend. My story is compiled from the archives and registers of the bishops, and partly from the letters of the martyrs themselves."[3]

Along with the emphasis on historical accuracy, religious biography developed gradually from a retelling of heroic deeds to a more intimate memoir, often by a biographer closely acquainted with the subject. One of the first important religious biographies published in America was Jonathan Edwards' moving remembrance of David Brainerd, a little-known missionary to the Indians, who died of tuberculosis while living with the Edwards family. Edwards prized his memory of Brainerd's exemplary love for God apart from all consideration of himself, and the publication of his essay on Brainerd's life was meant to share the impact of that faith more widely among the people of New England.

This effort to re-create the power of an individual's faith to move and change those who knew him became an increasingly important motivation for religious biographers. A long line of works, from Sereno Dwight's biography of Jonathan Edwards (1829) to the numerous "Life and Letters of . . ." biographies written by relatives and friends of distinguished clergymen, testifies to the importance of this genre in the United States during the nineteenth century.[4]

Psychology and Biography

For the contemporary biographer, however, it is not enough to study the subject's faith from the outside. Depth psychology has led to a new awareness of the internal tensions and conflicts that shape a person's actions, and this awareness has created in turn a new form of historiography that goes beneath the surface of actions to explore the motivational forces that lead to courage, creativity, and fidelity. This new discipline, often called psychohistory or psychobiography, takes many forms, simply because there are many different psychological theories that researchers may employ in their historical studies. Many works in psychohistory build primarily on psychoanalytic theory. Others, like the five studies in this volume, seek to combine psychoanalytic insights on the development of individual personality with rigorous attention to the growth of the cognitive processes by which human knowing, valuing, and action are shaped.

Psychohistory approaches the records of the past not to discover the details of a subject's life, but to analyze the origins of the styles of work and intimate relationships that have distinguished this person from others. Freud himself applied the psychohistorical method to the life of Leonardo da Vinci.[5] The distinguished church historian Henry Preserved Smith introduced the method into religious studies in his 1913 article, "Luther's Early Development in the Light of Psycho Analysis."[6]

The method of the psychohistorian is more specific than that of the traditional biographer, who may approach a subject as critic, friend, successor, or apologist. The psychohistorian brings to the documents of a historical subject a specific analytic framework that would be used to understand a living patient, client, or subject of a psychological study. While the psychohistorian is as interested as other biographers in the details of a subject's life, he brings to these data an explicit commitment to an interpretative framework that has been tested and perfected in the professional study of many other lives, ordinary and extraordinary, in the course of clinical practice or psychological research.

Erik Erikson's studies of Luther and Gandhi are perhaps the best examples of the psychohistorical method.[7] In an extended career as a clinical psychoanalyst, Erikson formulated a theory of *psychosocial development* to describe how people achieve stable, adult personalities through mastering the inevitable challenges of life. Erikson identified eight stages in the human life cycle—eight challenges from birth to old age and death—which must be met and mastered in every life. According to ego development theory, the human personality is faced with a series of tests imposed both by the social environment and by the biological requirements of growth, development, and aging. The young child must establish a sense of personal security, which Erikson calls "basic trust," making it possible for him to live apart from the constant presence of the mother, but with confidence in the mother's availability to meet the need for food and care. Adolescents must establish themselves in another way: by finding an identity that will allow them to emerge into adulthood as responsible persons and that will not allow them to lose themselves in the multiple roles they are called to play. The elderly have a different task. Their need is to maintain the adult integrity they have established in the face of physical decline and reduced responsibilities to work and family.[8]

A theory of psychosocial development like Erikson's proves its worth in therapeutic work. Though lacking the kind of empirical "proof" that relies upon controlled experiments and statistical analyses, it does provide a powerful system of concepts for mapping relationships between experiences in childhood or infancy and the struggles a person may encounter at later points in life. Significantly, Erikson's theory also makes advances over previous psychoanalytic theories of development in its effort systematicaly to take account of the interaction of the growing person with the social structures and cultural patterns around him. Based on cross-cultural studies as well as his clinical practice, Erikson's conception of the life-cycle provides a rich model for guiding biographical research.

In his biographical studies Erikson suggests that the same developmental model that helps one understand a patient in a clinic can help one understand the young monk, Martin, who falls in a faint in the choir, and why this same reticent scholar finds an unexpected and passionate release for his energies in lecturing on the power of faith. "In some periods of history," Erikson wrote at the beginning of *Young Man Luther,* "and in some phases of his life cycle, man needs (until we invent something better) a new ideological orientation as surely and sorely as he must have air and food. I will not be ashamed, then, even as I analyze what is analyzable, to display sympathy and empathy with a young man who (by no means lovable all of the time) faced the problems of human *existence* in the most forward terms of his era."[9]

Obviously, the psychological theory employed to shape a

historical analysis is at once the biographer's greatest resource and potentially his greatest weakness. Because the psychobiographer is looking for evidence that indicates internal tensions and unconscious motivations, he may stress statements and actions that seem less significant to historians concerned with external events. Because the psychobiographer judges evidence in part by its fit in a theoretical context, he may see plausibility in third-hand stories and fragmentary quotations that the pure documentary evidence will not support. Quarrels over historical evidence between the psychohistorian and his more traditional counterparts are therefore all but inevitable.

The greater danger for the psychobiographer, however, is that the theoretical model may not be adequate to help him grasp the reality he wants to explore. A tale of external events well told has its own intrinsic interest, but what good is a biographical exploration of a personality that misses the fundamental dynamics of the subject?

In some ways this danger is most apparent in biographical studies dealing with a person's religion or faith. For all that it has contributed to our understanding of religious dynamics and distortions, the Freudian tradition has had a hard time avoiding blatant or subtle tendencies to reduce faith to epiphenomenal status. Erikson's work marks a major turn toward treating matters of religion and faith as nonreducible, central dimensions of personality. But what happens if we make the focus on faith the central concern of our inquiry into lives? What happens if we take faith seriously as the principle of meaning and unity in persons' lives and as the source of their animating courage and purpose? The structural-developmental theory of faith which informs the studies in this book tests these questions. We need a brief account of how the structural-developmental theory understands faith in order to clarify how these studies were written.

INTRODUCTION

The Structural-Developmental Approach to Faith

One striking characteristic of faith is that it is comprehensive. What seems to us fundamentally true is never confined to some tiny corner of life, and a statement of faith is never just a statement about oneself. Our faith encompasses all that we find dependable in ourselves and in our relationships with other people. Our faith concerns what has been true in all our experiences so far, and what we confidently expect or fervently hope will be true in all our experiences in the future. The theologian Julian Hartt describes the comprehensiveness of faith in this way:

> In the religious life we are at once struck by the pre-eminence of the belief that here at last the "sense for the whole" is gratified. . . . The religious life expresses the sense of being able to endure all things and to hope for the best because the power and goodness which sustain the world are here at hand to sustain me.[10]

Faith, understood in these terms, is obviously broader and more personal than the set of beliefs we share with others in a particular religious tradition. Our faith is marked in important ways because we are Jewish, Catholic, or Presbyterian, but in order to understand the structural-developmental model of faith we must begin to see how these historic traditions are taken up by persons as they grow and change and mature. We must think of faith as a human universal, a feature of the living, acting, and self-understanding of all human beings, whether or not they would claim to be "religious" in any traditional way.

The Research Project on Faith and Moral Development has attempted to understand faith as a human universal by identifying basic *structures* of faith that all human beings seem to share. A structure of faith is a formal description of the way faith functions in life. It is not a basic system of

17

beliefs that different people might hold in common; it is a way that the mind operates in reasoning or judging about whatever content it focuses on. These "operating rules"—these structures—are not conscious. Ordinarily, we are unaware of them and we cannot articulate or explain them in the way we might explain the content of our religious beliefs. Rather, structures are the implicit rules underlying consciousness. They are the patterned processes that organize our thoughts and values in particular ways, thereby informing our actions and responses in life.

The idea that our ability to organize experience depends on certain basic structures of knowing has been widely discussed in twentieth-century psychology. Swiss epistemologist Jean Piaget has conducted many experimental studies with children to discover how persons develop operational structures that enable us to work mathematical problems, manipulate objects in space, and make accurate judgments about time and motion. According to Piaget the structures of knowing and valuing emerge in persons in a predictable sequence of cognitive stages. A "stage," in the Piagetian sense, is an integrated set of operations which makes thought possible. It is a *style* of thinking which forms or shapes the child's knowledge and understanding. The child moves to a new stage when maturation makes it possible, and when new problems—which can't be dealt with in the operational patterns of the present stage—require solution. A stage transition means a revolution in the child's *way* of knowing and understanding.[11]

Piaget pioneered in analyzing the structures we employ in knowing situations of moral dilemma and choice. He studied how children, by stages, develop the ability to construct the perspectives of others. Lawrence Kohlberg's studies of moral development have done much to extend Piaget's method in this area. Kohlberg presents a sequence of stages in moral development that describe the operations of reasoning and judgment that people employ in making moral decisions.[12]

The comprehensive quality of faith suggests, however, that the operations Piaget and Kohlberg describe are part of a larger structuring activity.[13] Whatever particular difficulties we may be meeting, whatever personal encounters we are experiencing, we are aware of a need not only to master the requirements of this situation, but to fit these experiences and responses into a larger horizon of meaning in which all events occur.

We live in the midst of events that impinge upon us in many ways. We come to know ourselves in our encounters with other persons, and we learn to express our knowledge of the world and of ourselves in terms of a shared language of meaning and value that allows us to communicate our insights to others. Faith is the liminal awareness that we can relate to all these complex encounters as parts of a whole which itself has meaning, and which gives meaning to each of its parts. Better still, faith is the active intention to bring this way of relating to the task of giving order and coherence to the multiplicity of our experiences.

To have faith, then, is not primarily to hold certain beliefs about reality. To have faith is to engage all of life in relation to a unifying center of meaning and value. Belief in God, if it truly expresses faith, is more than an affirmation that God exists, or an idea about God's judgments and mercy. The beliefs that are part of our faith are what Julian Hartt calls "construing beliefs":

> A construing belief is rather more a *believing* than it is the finished product commonly suggested by *belief.* Thus a construing belief is an interpretation of some aspect of experience. But it may also be a program, a mandate, as it were for interpreting all of experience and the world. . . .

Take, for example, the belief that God is Creator of all things and Lord over all. . . . . This belief is a declaration of intention both to "see" all things as belonging to God and actually so to construe them. Here "construe" is more than a linguistic-intellectual activity. *It means an intention to relate to all things in ways appropriate to their belonging to God.*[14]

Of course, not every "construing belief" is explicitly a belief about God. Certainly many people would deny that they have a "faith" in ordinary terms, or they would deny that the structures of faith operative in their lives have anything to do with the God of traditional theism. Many others, as the prophets have always reminded us, affirm their belief in God while the real structures through which they construe the world operate on other terms altogether. In structural terms faith is a universal human activity giving form to our affirmations about our experience taken as a whole, whether in the form of a religious creed, or in a heroic refusal to believe; whether in an articulate summary of the ground of hope or in a preverbal trust that hope is valid.

It should be clear by now that faith in the structural-developmental sense is never a static, completed formula. Faith exists in activity, in the ways we use religious symbols, in the ways we express our loyalties and commitments, in the ways we form our human relationships. To understand faith as a structure is to think of it as a verb, as a way of *doing*, of *knowing*, a way of *committing* and thus of *being*.

The development of faith concerns changes not so much in *what* we believe as in *how* we believe, how we "construe" the whole of our experience, to use Hartt's term again. Clearly this sort of construction does not wait for us to develop the intellectual sophistication and verbal skills that allow educated adults to make articulate statements of faith. Faith is a human universal not only in the sense that everyone employs some structure of faith, but also in the sense that this structuring activity has its origins in the very beginning of life, as the infant, whose world comprises his own immediate needs, learns to depend on the nurturing maternal presence that provides security and calms the terrors of hunger and discomfort. The structural-developmental approach focuses on faith as a lifelong process in which the structures of faith emerge, evolve, and are transformed in interaction with persons and events that make up the world for us.

Stages in Faith

To provide an account of the transformations that faith undergoes in experience, the Research Project on Faith and Moral Development has undertaken open-ended, or "semi-clinical," interviews with approximately three hundred persons across the spectrum of age, race, sex, and religious identity. The sample was closely balanced between males and females and has included Catholics, Protestants, Jews, a few adherents of Eastern traditions, and a good representation of nonbelievers. The sample manifests ethnic and racial diversity, and we sought to make it representative with respect to social class and educational background.[15] It must be said, however, that the Research Project has not conducted cross-cultural research, and we are only beginning follow-up interviews with the original subjects to provide a longitudinal perspective. For these reasons, the stage descriptions that follow here must be taken as provisional and as subject to refinement and revision.

What emerges in the studies to date is that there are six basic structuring styles, six ways of going about composing and maintaining a meaningful faith orientation. These stage-like styles emerge in a developmental sequence ranging from early imaginative modes of composing meaning to later coordinations of widened imagination and critical reasoning. At each stage, faith has characteristic ways of appropriating the symbols and beliefs of religious traditions.

Because faith involves relationships—to the neighbor, to God, or to other transcending centers of value and power—matters of identity formation and ego-development are inherent parts of faith growth. Paralleling Erikson's eight-stage model of the human life cycle, the theory of faith development underscores the critical importance of our earliest experiences in providing a fund of basic trust or mistrust upon which later faith growth will either build, or which it will have to overcome. As in psychosocial growth, faith development proceeds by way of crises.

At the same time faith is a way of *knowing,* and the stage model of faith development bears important resemblances to the stages of development found in Piaget and Kohlberg. These stages are structural wholes that comprise the ways of thinking and valuing in faith that are available to a person at a given time. A stage description explains the kinds of approaches to issues of faith that are possible and that will be employed by a person at this stage of development. Both the theoretical concept of a structural stage and the data of the faith development interviews lead us to expect that a person's responses will reveal a dominant stage of development that tends to characterize that person's approach to faith taken as a whole. That is, different issues or dilemmas are usually engaged from the perspective of a single, dominant stage.

Occasional responses will show residues of an earlier stage of development or reveal attempts to shape responses at the next higher stage. For the most part, however, the responses will reflect the structure of one's present stage of development.

Structural-developmental stages fall in this sort of sequence because they represent a series of tasks for the developing person in which each new life challenge arises in part from the limits of previous faith solutions. Every successful consolidation of a structural-developmental stage creates new questions that could not even be raised before. One must adopt a way of appropriating the absolute authority of parental values and beliefs (faith stage 2) before one can be puzzled about apparent conflicts between different authorities (faith stage 3). It is sometimes necessary to conceive the dilemmas of experience in sharp, unequivocal contrasts (faith stage 4) before it is possible to reappropriate the truths of both sides in a paradoxical relationship (faith stage 5).

Because the ways of making sense of the world in faith arise in this sequential fashion, we can schematize the developmental process as a sequence of stages, and we can hypothesize that everyone who arrives in the later stages will have previously constructed the entire sequence of styles, carrying forward the capacities of each of the previous stages. Precocity may increase the speed of this passage, but it will not allow one to skip any of the stages.

The stages in Erikson's model of the life cycle follow a similarly invariant sequence and are coordinate with the structural-developmental stages at several points, but Erikson's stages are a psycho-social description of certain maturational challenges that must be met by all individuals in the course of their lives. Whether one deals well or badly with the adolescent task of identity building, one faces in due course the adult problems of intimacy. The progress through the stages is ineluctable, if not always successful, because the psychophysiological construction of the organism requires it. By contrast, each successive structural-

23

developmental stage represents a new set of problems that only arise upon the successful consolidation of one's thinking and acting at the previous stage. Progress through the structural-developmental stages is not inevitable; indeed, as we shall see, the achievement of the highest stages of faith development appears to be quite rare. In outline, the stages of faith development are:

Undifferentiated Faith

The infant unconsciously forms a disposition toward his world during a preconceptual, largely prelinguistic stage.

Trust, courage, hope, and love are fused in an undifferentiated way and contend with sensed threats of abandonment, inconsistencies, and deprivations in the environment. Though really a pre-stage, and largely inaccessible to empirical inquiry of the kind we pursue, the quality of mutuality and the strength of trust, autonomy, hope, and courage (or their opposites) developed in this phase underlie (or undermine) all that comes later in faith development.

Transition to stage 1 begins with the convergence of thought and language, opening up the use of symbols in speech and ritual-play.

Stage 1. Intuitive-Projective Faith

Fantasy and imitation characterize stage 1, in which the child can be powerfully and permanently influenced by the examples, moods, actions, and language of the visible faith of primal adults.

The stage most typical of the child of three to seven,[16] it is marked by a relative fluidity of thought patterns. The

24

child is continually encountering novelties for which no stable operations of knowing have been formed. The imaginative processes underlying fantasy are unrestrained and uninhibited by logical thought. In league with forms of knowing dominated by perception, imagination in this stage can produce long-lasting images and feelings (positive and negative) which later, more stable and self-reflective valuing and thinking will have to order and sort out. This is the stage of first self-awareness. The "self-aware" child is egocentric as regards the perspectives of others. Here we find first awareness of death and sex, and of the strong taboos by which cultures and families insulated those powerful areas.

The emergence of concrete operational thinking underlies the transition to stage 2. Affectively, the resolution of Oedipal issues or their submersion in latency are important accompanying factors. At the heart of the transition is the child's growing concern to *know* how things are and to clarify for himself or herself the bases of distinctions between what is real and what only seems to be.

Stage 2. Mythic-Literal Faith

In stage 2, persons begin to take on for themselves the stories, beliefs, and observances that symbolize belonging to their communities. Beliefs are appropriated with literal interpretations, as are moral rules and attitudes. Symbols are taken as one-dimensional and literal in meaning.

In this stage the rise of concrete operations leads to the curbing and ordering of the previous stage's imaginative composing of the world. The episodic quality of intuitive-projective faith gives way to a more linear, narrative construction of coherence and meaning. Story becomes the major way of giving unity and value to experience. This is the faith stage of the school child (though we sometimes find its structures dominant in adolescents and in adults). Marked by increased accuracy in taking the perspective of other persons, stage 2 composes a world based on reciprocal fairness and immanent justice based on reciprocity. The actors in its cosmic stories are full-fledged anthropomorphic "personalities." It can be affected deeply and powerfully by symbolic and dramatic materials, and can describe in endlessly detailed narrative what has occurred. Stage 2 does not, however, step back from the flow of its stories to formulate reflective, conceptual meanings. For this stage the meaning is both carried and "trapped" in the narrative.

The implicit clash or contradictions of stories leads to reflection on meanings. The transition to formal operational thought makes such reflection possible and necessary. Previous literalism breaks down; new "cognitive conceit" (Elkind) leads to disillusionment with previous teachers and teachings. Conflicts between authoritative stories (i.e., Genesis on creation versus evolutionary theory) must be faced. The emergence of mutual interpersonal perspective-taking ("I see you seeing me; I see me as you see me; I see you seeing me seeing you") creates the need for a more personal relationship with the unifying power of the ultimate environment.

Stage 3. Synthetic-Conventional Faith

The person's experience of the world now extends beyond the family. A number of spheres demand attention: Family, school or work, peers, street society and media, and perhaps religion. Faith must provide a coherent orientation in the midst of that more complex and diverse range of involvements. Faith must synthesize values and information; it must provide a basis for identity and outlook.

Stage 3 typically has its rise and ascendancy in adolescence, but for many adults it becomes a permanent equilibration. It structures the ultimate environment in interpersonal terms. Its images of unifying value and power derive from the extension of qualities experienced in personal relationships. It is a "conformist" stage in the sense that it is acutely tuned to the expectations and judgments of significant others, and as yet does not have a sure enough grasp on its own identity and autonomous judgment to construct and maintain an independent perspective. While beliefs and values are deeply felt, they typically are tacitly held—the person "dwells" in them and the meaning world they mediate, but there has not been occasion to step reflectively outside them to examine them explicitly or systematically. At stage 3 a person has a "ideology," a more or less consistent clustering of values and beliefs, but he or she has not objectified it for examination, and in a sense is unaware of having it. Differences of outlook with others are experienced as differences in "kind" of person. Authority is located in the incumbents of traditional authority-roles (if perceived as personally worthy) or in the consensus of a valued, face-to-face group.

Factors contributing to the breakdown of stage 3 and to readiness for transition may include any one or more of the following: serious clashes or contradictions between valued authority sources; marked changes, by officially sanctioned leaders, of policies or practices previously deemed sacred and unbreakable (i.e., in the Catholic Church changing the Mass from Latin to the vernacular, or no longer requiring abstinence from meat on Friday); the encounter with experiences or perspectives that lead to

27

critical reflection on how one's beliefs and values have formed and changed, and on how "relative" they are to one's particular group or background.

Stage 4. Individuative-Reflective Faith

The movement from stage 3 to stage 4 is particularly critical, for it is in this transition that the late adolescent or adult must begin to take seriously the burden of responsibility for his or her own commitments, life-style, beliefs and attitudes. Where genuine movement toward stage 4 is underway the person must face certain unavoidable tensions: individuality versus being defined by a group or group membership; subjectivity and the power of one's strongly felt but unexamined feelings versus objectivity and the requirement of critical reflection; self-fulfillment or self-actualization as a primary concern versus service to and being for others; the question of being committed to the relative versus struggle with the possibility of an absolute.

This stage most appropriately takes form in young adulthood (but let us remember that many adults do *not* construct it and that for a significant group it emerges only in the mid-thirties or forties). This stage is marked by a double development. The self, previously sustained in its identity and faith compositions by an interpersonal circle of significant others, now claims an identity no longer defined by the composite of one's roles or meanings to others. To sustain that new identity it composes a meaning frame conscious of its own boundaries and inner connections and aware of itself as a worldview. Self (identity) and outlook (world view) are differentiated from those of others, and become acknowledged factors in the reactions, interpretations, and judgments one makes on the actions of the self and others. It expresses its intuitions of coherence in an ultimate environment in terms of an explicit system of meanings. Stage 4 typically translates symbols into conceptual meanings. This is a "demythologizing" stage. It is likely to attend minimally to unconscious factors influencing its judgments and behavior.

Restless with the self-images and outlook maintained by stage 4, the person ready for transition finds himself or herself attending to what may feel like anarchic and disturbing inner voices. Elements from a childish past, images and energies from a deeper self, a gnawing sense of the sterility and flatness of the meanings one serves—any or all of these may signal readiness for something new. Stories, symbols, myths, paradoxes from one's own or other traditions may insist on breaking in upon the neatness of the previous faith. Disillusionment with one's compromises, and recognition that life is more complex than stage 4's logic of clear distinctions and abstract concepts can comprehend, press one toward a dialectical and multileveled approach to life-truth.

Stage 5. Paradoxical-Consolidative Faith

This stage involves the integration into self and outlook of much that was suppressed or evaded in the interest of stage 4's self-certainty and conscious cognitive and affective adaptation to reality. This stage develops a "second naïveté" (Ricoeur), in which symbolic power is reunited with conceptual meanings. Here there must also be a new reclaiming and reworking of one's past. There must be an opening to the voices of one's deeper self. Importantly, this involves a critical recognition of one's *social* unconscious—the myths, ideal images, and prejudices built deeply into the self-system by virtue of one's nurture within a particular social class, religious tradition, ethnic group, or the like.

Unusual before mid-life, stage 5 knows the sacrament of defeat and the reality of irrevocable commitments and acts. What the previous stage struggled to clarify, in terms of the boundaries of self and outlook, this stage now makes porous and permeable. Alive to paradox and the truth in apparent contradictions, this stage strives to unify opposites in mind and experience. It generates and maintains vulnerability to the strange truths of those who are "other." Ready for closeness to that which is different and threatening to self and outlook (including new depths of experience in spirituality and religious revelation), this stage's commitment to justice is freed from the confines of tribe, class, religious community, or nation. And with the seriousness that can arise when life is more than half over, this stage is ready to spend and be spent for the cause of conserving and cultivating the possibility of others' generating identity and meaning.

Stage 5 can appreciate symbols, myths, and rituals (its own and others') because it has been grasped, in some measure, by the depth of reality to which they refer. It also sees the divisions of the human family vividly because it has been apprehended by the possibility (and imperative) of an inclusive community of being. But this stage remains divided. It lives and acts between an untransformed world and a transforming vision and loyalties. In some few cases this division yields to the call of the radical actualization that we call stage 6.

Stage 6. Universalizing Faith

This stage is exceedingly rare. The persons best described by this stage have generated faith compositions in which their felt sense of an ultimate environment is inclusive of all being. They become incarnators and actualizers of the spirit of a fulfilled human community.

They are "contagious" in the sense that they create zones of liberation from the social, political, economic, and ideological shackles we place and endure on human futurity. Living with felt participation in a reality that unifies and transforms the world, universalizers are often experienced as subversive of the structures (including religious structures) by which we sustain our individual and corporate survival, security, and significance. Many persons in this stage die at the hands of those whom they hope to change. Universalizers are often more honored and revered after death than during their lives. The rare persons who may be described by this stage have a special grace that makes them seem more lucid, more simple, and yet somehow more fully human than the rest of us. Their community is universal in extent. Particularities are cherished because they are vessels of the universal and are thereby valuable apart from any utilitarian considerations. Life is both loved and held to loosely. Such persons are ready for fellowship with persons at any of the other stages and from any other faith tradition.

The Faith Development Biographies

We have now completed this brief overview of the developmental stages of faith. These stages of the structural-developmental theory of faith, delineated from interviews with research subjects, provide another tool that is available to the psychobiographer who seeks to understand a historical subject through models based on present-day clinical or research data.

While the stages of faith development were emerging in our research, it occurred to the project director, Dr. James Fowler, that the structural-developmental perspective might be a particularly important tool for biographers engaged in the study of historical figures who were important because of their faith. At the same time, the experiment of attempting a plausible reconstruction of a great leader's faith, based on the structural-developmental model, seemed to provide an important opportunity to corroborate the findings of the interview research and especially to test the adequacy of the stage descriptions that we were building on the interview data.

Accordingly, in the fall of 1974 a group of graduate students at Harvard Divinity School, under Dr. Fowler's direction, made some preliminary studies in the application of the structural-developmental theory of faith to the problems of psychobiography with religious subjects. The results, while always interesting, were not uniformly successful. In the case of early historical subjects, who lived before the emergence of any of the forms of modern biography, there was seldom enough reliable biographical detail to allow a contemporary writer to reconstruct a pattern of development. While the psychobiographer has aims and methods rather different from those of the traditional biographer, successful psychobiography apparently requires a data base not only of extant literary works by the subject but also of reasonably reliable biographical studies assembled by other traditional methods. It became clear, too, that the absence of cross-cultural studies of faith development makes it extremely difficult for the biographer to apply the structural-development model in its present form to non-Western subjects. Finally, we found it quite difficult to apply the model successfully to living figures, whose work is often in transition and whose past—almost like that of some distant historical personage—often cannot be fully known.

Gradually, however, we identified a range of historical figures who could be successfully studied in this way. Western figures, men or women, who lived in the modern age—roughly since 1500—can be subjected to structural-developmental analysis, provided that we have enough of their writings or records of their conversations to know something of how they spoke and thought as well as what they did. The essays in this volume are refinements of the most successful biographical sketches that were prepared during the 1974 study. They provide an introduction to the use of the structural-developmental theory in biography and an indication of the variety that is possible even within the currently rather narrow limits of the method.

Each essay is intended to be a self-contained biography, a life history that can be read, if the reader wishes, without reference to the developmental theory that guided the writer. Yet each study also highlights aspects of the developmental theory and illustrates the importance of stage transitions in the faith of a major historical figure. Sometimes the study focuses on a particular stage in the subject's life. Anne Hutchinson's stage 4 conflict with the equally strong ideological rigidity of the Massachusetts Bay Colony is the center of chapter 3. In the case of Wittgenstein, critical attention is given to the stage 4/stage 5 transition in an effort to understand the remarkable philosophical contrasts between the "early" and "late" Wittgenstein. In the other cases—Malcom X, Bonhoeffer, and Pascal—the authors have attempted to give more or less uniform attention to the full course of their subject's development.

A brief concluding essay attempts to summarize what we have learned about faith in working on these studies. Before proceeding to the biographies, however, a few words of methodological introduction may be in order.

The structural-developmental biography uses the record of a person's life and words as a key to underlying structures of faith. Often, these structures appear most clearly in the way a subject uses words and symbols that have an explicit religious meaning. The structural-developmental biographer, however, is not only interested in the meaning that is given to the symbol. One looks also to the structuring of reality within which the symbol stands. A theologian reading Dietrich Bonhoeffer's essay "Protestantism Without Reformation"[17] might become intrigued by Bonhoeffer's understanding of the role of the "witness" in the Protestant tradition. He would then want to compare Bonhoeffer's idea with that of other contemporary theologians and trace its roots in the earlier history of the church. Our biographical study, however, will be concerned with the dynamics of the "witness" role in Bonhoeffer's own thought, and especially with the strong contrast between the role of the witness and the role of the exile. In structural terms, this strong dichotomizing of roles, ideals, and values is a clue to a stage 4 (individuative-reflective) structure of faith, while the relationships Bonhoeffer builds between the roles of witness and exile will be interpreted as signs of his own struggle to establish a stage 5 (paradoxical-consolidative) structure of faith to overcome the inner tensions he had engendered in his understanding of the German Church Struggle.

The structures of faith, of course, are not revealed exclusively in the use of religious ideas. We need to be alert to points at which faith is expressed in apparently nonreligious terms. For example, Wittgenstein's dichotomizing structures of stage 4 faith—here as yet unmodified by any second thought—appear quite plainly in the use of "ideals" in a letter to Bertrand Russell in 1914:

> You may be right in saying that *we ourselves* are not *so very different*, but our ideals could not be more so. And that's why we haven't been able and we shan't *ever* be able to talk about anything involving our value judgments without either becoming hypocritical or falling out. . . . Now perhaps,

you'll say, "Things have more or less worked, up to the present. Why not go on in the same way?" But I'm *too* tired of this constant sordid compromise.[18]

The substance of Wittgenstein's disagreement with Russell is not immediately clear from the quotation, but from the structural point of view the substance is less important than the clear indication that, for Wittgenstein at this stage, ideals mark divisions into sharply opposing positions, positions between which there can be no compromises.

Structures of faith may be revealed, then, in religious or nonreligious language. Indeed, if our theory is correct in understanding the stages of faith as structural wholes, there should be considerable similarity in the way a subject uses all of the language and symbols of basic commitments to ideals, values, political loyalties, and religious traditions.

The first step in preparing a structural-developmental biography of faith, then, is to identify a particular stage structure that dominates a person's thinking and speaking at some point in life. The stages of faith development that we have outlined then becomes a heuristic tool to guide our reconstruction of the changes in faith in the life of our subject. Beginning from a clearly established structure at one stage of development, we can proceed backward through time to marshal the evidence characterizing earlier faith stages, and we have a general description of the sorts of changes later in life that would be indicative of further faith development. The stages of faith development, in short, allow us to plot a trajectory in faith, a path that development is likely to follow and an indication of where we might find a historical subject struggling with the structures of his or her own faith in the context of the problems of the age.

In Pascal's *Pensées*, for example, we have a work of apologetic theology that had a major impact on the development of French literature and also represented a new departure in religious thought. By engaging in a presentation of the faith intended to win over the skeptical mind, and not merely to reduce it to silence, Pascal introduced a way of meeting the new secular, scientific culture with a style of Christianity that could not be easily dismissed as a relic of the superstitious past.

Developmental theory, however, sees behind the brilliant strategy and style of the *Pensées* to Pascal's own struggle to move beyond the dichotomized, world-rejecting faith of the Port Royal community that had become his spiritual home during the fourth stage of his own faith development. In the *Pensées*, Pascal reaches out to integrate in a genuine, if paradoxical, unity the many elements of his own genius: the scientific viewpoint; the analytical power of his mathematics; and the penetrating, disciplined, and self-effacing insights of his Christianity. In the easy, winning style of the fragments we also see—raised to a new level of importance—the persuasive powers of the young genius who not only invented a calculating machine but set about to advertise it.

The stage theory of faith development allows us to tie the story of a life together, to bridge the gap of years when records and recollections may be sparse, and to hold the projects of youthful enthusiasm in developmental continuity with the achievements of old age. Of course, this trajectory does not provide a causal explanation of the genius of a religious leader. It is not intended to do so. The structural-developmental theory is rather a model of the interaction between the problem-solving and experience-ordering structures of the human mind and the problems and possibilities that the mind finds before it in a particular historic and cultural setting. The structural-developmental approach can help us understand the creativity and freedom with which a genius of faith moves beyond the conventional truths of the age to experience problems that others do not yet see and develop answers that they have not dreamed.

Reconstructing that movement beyond conventional truths is the key to re-creating the impact of a life of faith. The studies in this book, like other stories of saints and heroes, are important because they show the creative power of faith. In the lives we present, we see not the fivefold repetition of a single pattern of development, but five of the myriad ways that hope and trust can be affirmed in life, five of the ways that faith has conquered despair and doubt.

1

Introduction

These trajectories in faith begin with a study that illustrates the complex interactions between faith and identity. The faith development of Malcolm X shows us a man who struggled with integrity for a faith that would free his powerful gifts for action in a world that for the most part rejected his person and threatened his dreams.

Faith cannot be simply the sum of a person's positive experiences in life. An adequate faith must also encompass the griefs and rejections that we feel. For Malcolm, this meant a search for a faith that could sustain a child's sense of being at home in a world where he was valued and given pride and hope, even after the child became a man, the home collapsed under the pressure of society's racism, and the boy's hope and pride were dashed on a white teacher's admonitions to be "realistic" about "being a nigger."

The outline of Malcolm's pilgrimage of faith is well known: His early adult attempts to make a place for himself as a "hustler" and small-time criminal landed him in prison. There he encountered for the first time the Nation of Islam, whose faith proclaimed the worth of that identity which white society most vigorously denied, the identity of a black man seeking to take control of his own life. Malcolm Little became Malcolm X, chief spokesman for the movement that awakened millions, Muslim and non-Muslim, to the proud reality of black humanity. Then, toward the end of his life, following a real pilgrimage to Mecca, Malcolm had a new experience of Islam as a universal faith, and he began to envision his own faith in new ways that could encompass the experience of all races.

"The Pilgrimage in Faith of Malcolm X" points to the complexities of this new vision. Written originally as a lecture for an audience primarily of black Christians at Gammon Theological Seminary in Atlanta, Dr. Fowler's essay is a white theologian's attempt to address the racial experience that both unites the black American Christians and Malcolm X and separates them from his own white churchmanship. At the same time it acknowledges the community of Christian faith that makes the racial particularism of Malcolm's Nation of Islam problematic for many Christians, black and white.

What emerges most clearly in this study is the fact that there is no straight and easy path from childhood's trust to the more complex and responsible patterns of adult faith. The capacity to integrate the paradoxes and partial truths of human experience is founded in a secure and flexible identity for oneself, an identity that must sometimes be forged by a powerful self-assertion against a hostile or indifferent world.

James W. Fowler is the Director of the Research Project on Faith and Moral Development, and associate professor of theology and human development at Candler School of Theology, Emory University.

The Pilgrimage
in Faith of Malcolm X

James W. Fowler

Seen simultaneously as a saint, a martyr, and a symbol of revolution, Malcolm X is coming to be understood better in death than he ever was in life. Malcolm's life constitutes a consummately important subject of reflection for anyone who is interested in the development of genuine faith. I propose to examine what we know of Malcolm's life in regard to the development and expression of his faith. In giving this account I shall use our stages in faith development to organize and clarify the course of Malcolm's pilgrimage. At the same time I will use the extraordinary content of his life and growth as an example that demonstrates the concrete meaning and heuristic power of the developmental stage theory. In this account, I have tried to avoid distortion, overinterpretation, and the temptation to force-fit the data of this man's life too readily into the categories of a present schema. Where I have failed, I hope and expect to be corrected. Where I have succeeded, I hope others will be illumined and inspired, as I have been, by the sensitivity and spiritual depth, as well as the courage and moral passion, of a great, complex, non-Christian black American.

Malcolm's Childhood

The first three or four years of life, Erik Erikson tells us, are of tremendous importance for all that comes thereafter in the way of faith and identity. Even in the first year—a year in which more actual development occurs than in any other comparable time period—a fundmental disposition toward one's world and one's place in it is being formed. The first life-defining conflict the infant must resolve is that between a *fundamental trust* in the reliability and generosity of his little world, or a *basic mistrust* based on the perception that his world is arbitrary, unreliable, and not committed to his continuance and well-being. This fundamental faith attitude is shaped on the basis of the baby's *inference* from the way the environment—particularly embodied in the mother or the primary caring one—works to meet his needs and to nurture his growth. The baby's growing sense of trust is preverbal, preconceptual, and presymbolic. It is communicated primarily through the complex language of body contact, gestural rituals, and the mutual fit of infantile need and the parental need to be needed.[1]

Malcolm's *Autobiography*[2] tells us little about this earliest stage in his development of faith and identity. (In the stage theory, this corresponds to what we have called undifferentiated faith—stage 0.) But we get from his account the picture of a home where both mother and father are present. They are forceful, self-directing people. They live in a home that the father had built with his own hands. There are other, older children. From the beginning, however, this familial circle is surrounded by a hostile environment that could without warning shatter the stillness of the night with shots and broken windows and color the night air with flames and white-robed hatred. Malcolm's earliest vivid memory was of such a night:

> I remember being suddenly snatched awake into a frightening confusion of pistol shots and shouting and smoke and flames. My father had shouted and shot at two white men who had set the fire and were running away. Our home was

burning down around us. We were lunging and jumping and tumbling all over each other trying to escape. My mother, with the baby in her arms, just made it into the yard before the house crashed in, showering sparks. I remember we were outside in the night in our underwear, crying and yelling our heads off. The white police and firemen came and stood around watching as the house burned down to the ground.[3]

For Malcolm the preconscious faith of earliest childhood had to accommodate this threat of arbitrary violence, but it also had powerful models of autonomy, courage, and the hope of a better future for a transformed people. Malcolm's father, a Baptist preacher, one-eyed, the father of six children before Malcolm and of four after him, was a large and physically powerful man. While saving money to establish his own store, he spent much of his time between Sundays organizing for Marcus A. Garvey's Universal Negro Improvement Association. In retrospect Malcolm was to remember sharply contrasting feelings toward his father's leadership in the Baptist churches and his work as an organizer for the Garvey movement.

He [Malcolm's father] never pastored in any regular church of his own; he was always a "visiting preacher." I remember especially his favorite sermon: "that little *black* train is a-comin' . . . an' you better get all your business right! . . . My brother Philbert, the one just older than me, loved church, but it confused and amazed me. I would sit goggle-eyed at my father jumping and shouting as he preached, with the congregation jumping and shouting behind him, their souls and bodies devoted to singing and praying. Even at that young age, I just couldn't believe in the Christian concept of Jesus as someone divine. And no religious person until I was a man in my twenties—and then in prison—could tell me anything. I had very little respect for most people who represented religion.[4]

42

There is a clear suspicion of his father in the role of the "whooping" preacher, and some suggestion that even then Malcolm sensed in it a form of economically necessary prostitution for his father. On the other hand, Malcolm's respect and imagination were vastly kindled by the Garvey UNIA meetings to which he went with his father:

> To the best of my remembrance, it was only me that he sometimes took with him to the Garvey UNIA meetings which he held quietly in different people's homes. There were never more than a few people at any one time—twenty at most. But that was a lot, packed into someone's living room. I noticed how differently they all acted, although they were the same people who jumped and shouted in church. But in these meetings both they and my father were more intense, more intelligent and down to earth. It made me feel the same way.[5]

My studies in faith development convince me that the ages four to six or seven are often extremely crucial in providing the foundation for adult faith. Though the child does not cognitively sort out and understand what is going on, he is open to impression by the images, moods, gestures, and works of piety of adults who are primally related to him. Negatively, where there are no primal adults whose lives are visibly devoted to values of some transcendant import, the chance is strengthened that the growing person will merely accommodate himself to the world of surface reality and be less likely later to generate a vision in which both he and it could be different and better. The drive to world-transformation often has its prime rootage in this stage, where imagination is exploding and where imitation of significant adults and speculation on one's future role become matters of earnest play. We have called this stage 1, intuitive-projective faith.

Malcolm speaks again of the Garvey meetings led by his father:

I can remember hearing of "Adam driven out of the garden into the caves of Europe," "Africa for the Africans," "Ethiopians, Awake!" And my father would talk about how it would not be much longer before Africa would be completely run by Negroes—"by black men," was the phrase he always used. "No one knows when the hour of Africa's redemption cometh. It is in the wind. It is coming. One day, like a storm, it will be here."

He continues,

I remember seeing the big shiny photographs of Marcus Garvey that were passed from hand to hand. My father had a big envelope of them that he always took to these meetings. The picures showed what seemed to me millions of negroes thronged in a parade behind Garvey riding in a fine car; a big black man dressed in a dazzling uniform with gold braid on it, and he was wearing a thrilling hat with tall plumes. I remember hearing that he had black followers not only in the United States but all around the world, and I remember how the meetings always closed with my father saying, several times and the people chanting after him, "Up, you mighty race, you can accomplish what you will!"[6]

Discipline came primarily from Malcolm's mother—the discipline of punishment of wrongdoing. (He sometimes suspected discipline was made harder on him than the others because his light complexion so fully mirrored the blood of his white rapist grandfather, which she had transmitted to him. His father, very dark, seemed to favor Malcolm above the other children.) Malcolm got other discipline from his mother—religious seriousness and discipline about what one eats or does not eat on principle; discipline about cleanliness and pride; and the gentle discipline of making and caring for a garden of his own:

One thing in particular that I remember made me feel grateful toward my mother was that one day I went and asked her for my own garden, and she did let me have my own little plot. I loved it and took care of it well. I loved especially to grow peas. I was proud when we had them on our table. I would pull out the grass in my garden by hand when the first little blades came up. I would patrol the rows on my hands and knees for any worms and bugs, and I would kill and bury them. And sometimes when I had everything straight and clean for my things to grow, I would lie down on my back between two rows, and I would gaze up in the blue sky at the clouds moving and think all kinds of things.[7]

Rarely have I heard so pure and whole an account of an experience of religious transcendence. In the small confines of a ground-space entrusted to him by a demanding but loving mother, a little boy achieves an impressive blend of work and play, of care and abandonment. Here is the nurture of growing things and the careful destruction (with proper burial rituals) of intruding parasites. Out of this matrix of freedom and self-control comes a unity with the powers of growth and with the overarching mystery of an infinite sky. This, if we had eyes to see it and grace to achieve it, constitutes a model of transcendent happiness.

The otherwise insightful study of Malcolm's religious development given by Eugene Bianchi in his book *The Religious Experience of Revolutionaries,* is marred by the fact that he fails to take seriously enough the powerful rootage of Malcolm's adult faith in these experiences and relations of his earliest childhood.[8]

We know that Malcolm's father was brutally killed when Malcolm was six. His mother was left with the responsibility for eight children. Malcolm and his brothers and sisters had to watch the at first gradual, and then subsequently rapid, destruction of their mother's ability to cope under the inhumane and economically inadequate ministrations of the welfare system. In the pit of the depression, when he was about ten, Malcolm reports:

Something began to happen. Some kind of psychological deterioration began to eat away our pride. Perhaps it was the constant tangible evidence that we were destitute. We had known other families who had gone on relief. We had known without anyone in our home ever expressing it that we had felt prouder not to be at the depot where the free food was passed out. And now, we were among them. At school, the "on relief" finger suddenly was pointed at us, too, and sometimes it was said aloud.[9]

Bianchi's study of Malcolm's religious development seems to pick up at about this point. What he describes as the first period in Malcolm's faith pilgrimage seems to have begun with the petty thieving of fruit and other food to help feed the family. Bianchi describes this first period in this way: "The first stage, of his early youth and young adulthood, was characterized by the enslavement of a criminal hustler to the destructive values of white America."[10]

From our studies in faith development I am led to believe that adequate understanding of Malcolm's pilgrimage has to take more into account than Bianchi does. After his father's death there seem to have been four years in which the family stayed intact, maintaining its values and dignity even though the belt had to be drawn in. Peas and other vegetables, I suspect, grew in those summers as well. Though the going was tougher, my guess is that the childish memories of his father's faith in Garvey's vision, his father's powerful articulation of the promise of an empowered black race, continued to enliven the fantasies and speculations of the lanky boy who sometimes lay down between the rows to look up at the sky "and think all kinds of things." The energizing myth of a coming black rule in Africa, and of a realizable black manhood in America, must have taken on added sharpness because of the father's death. Though everyday school life made the revelation of these myths and dreams dangerous, Malcolm must have nurtured them and kept them burning like a hidden bull's-eye lantern within. I suspect there was in Malcolm, as we find in many of our respondents in the ages of seven to ten or eleven, a fairly coherent (if very private) set of stories or mythic images by which he bound together a view of the world, and of himself in it, which held promise, beauty, heroism, and perhaps sacrificial leadership. We have called this stage 2, mythic-literal faith—the stage at which Malcolm's ground trust in the coherence of things and his belief in the possibility of his own and of his race's "somebodiness" were sustained. With remembered symbols of his father's faith, and with a store of memories and some continuing experience of a oneness with the powers of growth and wholesomeness in nature, Malcolm's faith endured.

Malcolm's Adolescence and Young Manhood

What did Malcolm the teen-ager do with the legitimate anger and suspicion, the grief and despair that, with basic trust, were also the legacies of his childhood? We can be sure that in both conscious and unconscious ways they were part of his faith. Malcolm gradually would become more aware of the dead-end quality of most of the conventionally sanctioned roles society had to offer him. It is little wonder that this precocious and extraordinarily energetic young man should begin to gravitate toward roles and self-images that are defined negatively by the majority society, but that allowed him to develop his leadership and entrepreneurial drives and to strike real blows against the oppressive majority. What Malcolm came later to see was how much anger against himself—absorbed unconsciously from his life experiences and the hostile environment—there was in his behavior during this period. Listen to Erik Erikson speaking about his concept of *negative identity,* a matter that can become crucial at adolescence:

> The *negative identity* is the sum of all those identifications and identity fragments which the individual had to submerge in himself as undesirable or irreconcilable or by which atypical individuals and marked minorities are made to feel "different." In the event of aggravated crises, an individual (or indeed a group) may despair of the ability to contain these negative elements in a positive identity. A specific rage can be aroused wherever identity development loses the promise of a traditionally assured wholeness: thus an as yet uncommitted delinquent may become a criminal.[11]

We see an interesting Malcolm at fifteen. He has traveled from Mason, Michigan, to Boston to visit his older stepsister Ella, a proud and able woman who inspired him to hold high expectations of himself. Back in Mason he had been elected president of his seventh-grade class. Now he is near the top of his eighth-grade class, competing for top honors with a white girl and boy. This is to be his last year of formal schooling. He is washing dishes in the afternoons, moving from pillar to post in foster homes; his brothers and sisters are scattered all over the country. His mother is in a state mental hospital—the victim of overwork, poverty, and what Malcolm saw as a systematic effort by a succession of social workers to separate the children from her and to undermine their confidence in her sanity.

Looking back later he saw as symbolic a conversation with a white eighth-grade teacher, a man who had seemed to like him, and who fancied himself an adviser to his students.

> He told me, "Malcolm, you ought to be thinking about a career. Have you been giving it thought?" The truth is, I hadn't. I never have figured out why I told him, "Well, yes sir, I've been thinking I'd like to be a lawyer." . . .
> Mr. Ostrowski looked surprised, I remember, and leaned back in his chair and clasped his hands behind his head. He

kind of half smiled and said, "Malcolm, one of life's first needs is for us to be realistic. Don't misunderstand me now. We all like you here, you know that. But you've got to be realistic about being a nigger. A lawyer—that's no realistic goal for a nigger."[12]

At a time when most of the boys we interview are working out their own individual variants of what we have called stage 3, synthetic-conventional faith, Malcolm came face to face with the fact that there was no sponsorship in Mason, religious or otherwise, for his giftedness and self-conscious blackness. The only conventional faith or identity white America seemed ready to offer him was a choice between sterile, whitewashed mediocrity and the demanding, ultimately self-destructive, negative identity of a borderline criminal. After a period in Boston this set of options began to clarify itself in Malcolm's experience. He moved gradually but steadily in the direction that seemed to offer him the only outlets for his virtuosity and his drives. One of his sponsors in his passage to the life of a hustler gave him a formula that he, years later, would recall as a fitting expression of the negative principle of faith on which he began to operate: "The main thing you've got to remember is that everything in the world is a hustle."[13]

Synthetic-conventional faith represents a way of interpreting and orienting oneself in life that enables one to hold together the various spheres of work, play, intimacy, leisure, and worship or valuing. A stage beyond the mythic-literal, it comes to grips with some of life's ambiguities and polarities that the earlier stage does not need to recognize. These polar tensions or ambiguities are resolved by appeal to tradition, to authority, or to a communal consensus. It is characteristic of this stage that in it one is still primarily dependent upon the formal or informal beliefs of a valued community for basic refercences concerning faith and identity. Many adolescents today pick up counter-culture language and ideas, and sound as though they are rooted in anything but conventional communities. But when one analyzes the structure of their thinking and probes for the grounds of their beliefs, one discovers that their *real* faith seems to be a blend of a familial-conventional outlook and some accretions to it of a conventionalized counter-culture outlook, mediated and held up by the media and their peers.

In contrast to this typical experience of white (and apparently of many black) teen-agers, Malcolm's intelligence and experiences were such that his creativity and drives—and his angers at the white world and at himself—could find expression only in conventionally negative roles. Bianchi insightfully speaks of this period in Malcolm's life as *irreligious,* "not because (he) spurned churches and gained the nickname 'Satan,' but because of his stunting of his own growth toward freedom in community."[14] It would be more accurate to say that he became "irreligious" because of the stunting of his growth toward freedom by the obstacles of a racist society.

As I reflect on Malcolm's situation, it seems that his years in the streets—as hustler, pusher, and thief—must be seen as a kind of stage 3 phase. It seems fair to say that during this period, more than any other in his life, Malcolm was acting on unexamined and fatalistically accepted values. Barred from more constructive channels, he poured his tremendous energies and drives into the struggle for survival and significance in the tough, materialistic life of the streets. Malcolm's situation—and that of many others like him— is a searing reflection of what W. E. B. DuBois had seen clearly many years before.[15] When racist patterns of law, economics, and politics block the way to human fulfillment, and when conventional religion sponsors only a partial caricature of manhood or womanhood, the person of clear vision and unclear opportunity has little alternative but to attack the society's underbelly, bleeding it of its own worst creations and choking in its offal. Malcolm's stage 3 faith had to be primarily negative in character.

The Conversion to the Lost-Found Nation

It required a powerful kind of religious encounter to reawaken the deeply buried residues of Malcolm's earlier trust in himself and in possible world coherence and meaning. It would take the enlivening spark of a new total view of history and of the place of black people in it to penetrate the grief-caused and experience-confirmed cynicism that Malcolm had been living out. In prison, when his life was at rock-bottom, Malcolm encountered the teaching of the man he came to call the honorable Elijah Muhammad. Mediated by family members and by the letters of Elijah Muhammad himself, the new vision quickly captivated him. Once the transforming power of the new teaching began to work in him, Malcolm said it took him a week to make the crucial symbolic step of getting into the position of prayer:

> The hardest test I ever faced in my life was praying. You understand. My comprehending, my believing the teachings of Mr. Muhammad had only required my mind's saying to me "That's right" or "I never thought of that." But bending on my knees to pray—that *act*—well, that took me a week. . . . For evil to bend its knees, admitting its guilt, to implore the forgiveness of God, is the hardest thing in the world.[16]

But when he was over that hurdle, he said, things changed quickly:

> I still marvel at how swiftly my previous life's thinking pattern slid away from me, like snow off a roof. It is as

though someone else I knew of had lived by hustling and crime. I would be startled to catch myself thinking in a remote way of my earlier self as another person.[17]

Malcolm's conversion to the Lost-Found Nation occurred during his twenty-seventh and twenty-eighth years. In his commitment to this religious movement Malcolm was what we would call a "totalizer." For him everything came to center in the authority and teaching of Elijah Muhammad and in the internal morality of the Nation. Malcolm's wholehearted commitment, his native intelligence and leadership qualities, his prodigious energy, and his genius for communication combined to accelerate his rise to leadership in the Nation.

His new faith exhibited all the qualities characteristic of a totalizing, stage 4, individuative-reflective faith. It provided clear, sharp boundaries of inclusion and exclusion, it dichotomized the world into the saved and the damned; it provided ethical guidelines that required discipline and self-sacrifice; and it demanded total subordination of individual will and autonomy to the authority of Allah—as mediated through his messenger. As Malcolm's hold on the new faith became more secure, and as he demonstrated both his ability and his commitment to Elijah Muhammad, he was given ample leeway to exert his own leadership and to develop his own initiatives. (Parenthetically, we might add that Malcolm's self-education, which began in the Charles Street Jail in Boston and proceeded at a prodigious rate during his jail years and after his conversion, eventually made him one of the most widely read men of his time.) Under Malcolm's leadership new mosques were founded at a quickening rate. As the tempo of racial confrontation accelerated in the late fifties and early sixties, he wanted the Lost-Found Nation to move into the streets and give organizing leadership to urban and ghetto blacks. Both the deterministic theology of the Muslim movement and the inherent conservatism of its leadership operated, however, as constraints on Malcolm's desire to make a political and economic impact beyond the Nation's boundaries. Bianchi provides a useful summary of the deterministic doctrines of the Muslims and of their implications for social change:

> Allah is a deterministic divinity outside of history, who as an all-knowing and all powerful ruler, will impose his judgment on white devils by future intervention in history. "Allah" expresses a fatalism about the present and the future. Whoever goes against Allah's truth will be cursed in this life, and "everything is written" according to which the future is set. . . . Human effort to bring about change (is) very secondary.[18]

There is considerable evidence that Malcolm was restless with the other-worldly ethics and the exclusivistic emphasis of the Muslim movement several years before his separation from it. But there is little to lead us to believe that he anticipated leaving the movement. It appears, rather, that he hoped to transform it from within and to demonstrate to Mr. Muhammad, by his successes in relating to a widening group of non-Muslim audiences, that the Nation had both opportunities and responsibilities for leadership beyond its own borders.

Separation and Beyond: The Last Stage

The story of Malcolm's separation from the Nation is a complex one. Here we do not need to examine it in full detail.[19] For our purposes the separation is important primarily as a major element in Malcolm's transition to what seems to have been, in the last years of his life, an emergent stage 5, paradoxical-consolidative faith outlook.

Between 1961 and 1963 Malcolm attracted national and international attention as a Muslim leader. He often crisscrossed the U.S. three and four times a week helping with the establishment of new mosques. By 1963 he was second only to Senator Barry Goldwater in demand as a speaker on college and university campuses. An interview with him in *Playboy* magazine in 1963, as well as earlier studies of the Muslims in which he played a prominent role, had made him a better known figure in the U.S. than even Elijah Muhammad. More than most Muslims, Malcolm had occasion to interact with the non-Muslim world and with the world of "white devils." Malcolm immensely enjoyed his speaking on campuses. During those years, he was, in effect, functioning as two different men. In the mosques he was preacher and church statesman. There he purveyed the religious beliefs and historical-eschatological mythology of the Nation with unequaled skill. On the campuses he was the provocative, prophetic social critic, confronting white America with its racism and embodying a steely black confidence and courage, both with unparalleled force.

Jealousy and the fear that he might undercut the absolute authority of orthodoxy seem to have played prominent roles in hardening the hearts of Muslim officialdom against him. In 1962 and 1963, while his publicity in non-Muslim media increased rapidly, in official Muslim publications he was mentioned less and less. There was another issue that increased tensions between Malcolm and the Muslim leadership. Malcolm the puritan, the all-or-nothing true believer, came to suspect that Mr. Muhammad himself had not lived up to the strict Muslim sexual code he enjoined to others. Convinced that the scandal, if it became public, might wreck the Nation, Malcolm confronted Mr. Muhammad and shared his fears with a number of his fellow ministers. This resulted in a gradual but inexorable isolation of Malcolm in the Muslim world. At the top a decision apparently had been made that he had to be silenced and his influence neutralized.

Malcolm resisted seeing what finally became unmistakably obvious in late November of 1963, when he was suspended from speaking publicly for ninety days by Elijah Muhammad. During that enforced silence he had to embrace his worst fears and suspicions. He had been betrayed by the man whom he believed to be semi-divine and whom he credited with having made him all that he was. He had been betrayed and excluded by fellow ministers, many of whom he had recruited and helped train.

It is difficult to tell who in fact betrayed whom. Certainly Malcolm intended no treachery and consciously had no intention of supplanting Mr. Muhammad. But his drive, his intelligence, his broadened horizons, curious mind, and outspoken disregard for meliorating public relations all made him increasingly a threat and danger within the Muslim nation. When a son cannot consciously will to break with a powerful, semi-divine father, he *can* set in motion a pattern of effectiveness and widening autonomy that will eventually require the father to try to curb him, thus necessitating and justifying a break.

Journalist Peter Goldman—neither a psycho-historian nor a theologian—writes about Malcolm's separation from Muhammad. Goldman's book appeared after I had written and delivered an earlier draft of this chapter as a lecture. I found in it an authoritative confirmation of what I had previously concluded about Malcolm. Here I quote from several passages in his book which show us Malcolm in transition from stage 4 to stage 5:

> His transformation this time was as profound as his conversion to Islam in prison but not nearly so sudden or melodramatic; it happened as process, not revelation, and it

55

ran out over weeks and months of trial and error, discovery and disappointment.[20] . . .

When he departed the Nation, Malcolm left some of his certainties behind; the White Question was no longer quite so simple for him as it had been in the days when Yacubs' History answered all one's questions about the origin of species. Even then, Malcolm knew from his almost daily encounters with whites that they were not nearly so terrifying an enemy as Satan. . . .[21] To have reached a point where one lost sight of color was, for a Black Muslim, to have sunk in error. Malcolm understood this and resisted the consequences as long as he could; he clung to the letter of his faith, in the classic way of priests in doubt, and dealt with his heretical tendencies by repressing them. But his last years in the Nation had eroded his belief, and his exile freed him from the necessity of believing.

Goldman concludes:

> He was drifting free, open and light-sensitive and suscepti-
> ble. He remained a religious man, a true believer cut loose
> from one system of faith and looking for another that would
> more nearly suit his experience of the world and would offer
> him religious legitimacy as well.[22]

Malcolm sought for his new faith orientation in true Islam. In the last year of his life he made two pilgrimages to Mecca. On each trip he spent considerable time in the Middle East and then made triumphant trips to Nigeria, Ghana, and other African nation-states. Evidence that he self-consciously rejected the stage 4 qualities of his earlier faith show up in his comments about his first trip to Mecca and Africa:

> My thinking had been opened up wide in Mecca. In the long
> letters I wrote to friends, I tried to convey to them my new
> insights into the American black man's struggle and
> problems, as well as the depths of my search for truth and

justice. "I've had enough of someone else's propaganda," I had written to these friends. "I'm for truth, no matter who it is for or against. I'm a human being first and foremost, and as such I'm for whoever and whatever benefits humanity as a whole."[23]

Conclusion

In this transition to a new expression of his faith, Malcolm X—previously Malcolm Little, "Homeboy," "Detroit Red," "Satan,"—once again took a new name: El-Hajj Malik El Shabazz. The frantic rush of his last months—the growing realization that violent death was closing in on him—left him no time to work out his faith position and the politics of the African and Afro-American coalition he envisioned. In his cautious new openness his more militant followers saw him as having sold out to whites and to the established civil rights movements. The white press, on the other hand, quickly became bored with the new, less quotable, less absolute Malcolm. The bitter fight with the old Muslims hung like a rotting albatross around his neck. When death finally came, after his home was bombed and after weeks of threats and ominous near misses, it sealed the impossibility of forty-year-old Malcolm's completing the transition to a faith and style of leadership that would have fit the person he had become and was becoming.

Continually portrayed by the American press as a fomenter of violence and as a pernicious enemy of peace, El-Hajj Malik El-Shabazz did not live to see a United States in which his ideal of serving truth and justice wherever they led him could be made operative. The patterns of fear and prejudice, buttressed in economic and political structures, gave no leeway or resonance for the expanded sense of human brotherhood that had begun to take root in his mind and imagination. Had there been time, and had there been a willingness on the part of the media and of white America to hear and understand him, his stage 5 commitment to a truth that transcends while including the particularities of his own experience might have made a powerful impact for good upon us all.

2

Introduction

Anne Hutchinson's story parallels the stories of many women in the early seventeenth century. Born in England in 1591, she came to the New World with her husband and family to seek a better civil order and a purer religious community. Like the other women of colonial Boston, she took her faith seriously, as a matter of regular study, earnest conversation, and daily practice.

Unlike the others, however, Anne Hutchinson carried her religious quest beyond the conventional limits that Puritan society established for women's religion. Her earnest conversations grew beyond the ladies' hearthside chats to become instructive discussions of theology for dozens of men and women. Her study moved beyond reverent attention to the opinions of the Cambridge-trained clergymen, to an outspoken defense of her own religious views and a trust in her own faith experience that was stronger than the rigid framework of Puritan theology. Because of the controversy sparked by her unconventional beliefs, we have a record of the faith development of Anne Marbury Hutchinson; the quieter faith of the Puritan wives and daughters, who listened to her words and shared her experiences, went unrecorded. Theology in Boston in 1637 was regarded as a subject exclusively for the minds and pens of men.

To that degree, there is something strikingly contemporary about Anne Hutchinson's controversy, something that is more easily seen when the analytical framework of developmental theory and the insights of the psychology of religion are applied to the records that have survived the centuries. The terminology of the "antinomian controversy" in the New England churches is obscure to us, and the points at issue are difficult to comprehend, but we know well enough what happens when a minority group oversteps the bounds assigned to them and begins to claim for their experience the universal validity and redemptive power that the prevailing authorities have reserved for their own ideas. A developmental study of Anne Hutchinson introduces us to the subtle interaction of historical and personal change that allowed one powerful woman's transition to a post-conventional faith to shake the rigid structure of religious convention throughout the Massachusetts Bay Colony.

Katherine Ann Herzog is a writer, teacher, and student of women's religious movements. Her efforts to reconstruct the faith of Anne Hutchinson led her not only to the numerous modern studies of women's role in seventeenth-century religion but also to the manuscript resources of the Massachusetts Historical Society.

Vision and Boundaries:
The Faith of Anne Hutchinson

Katherine Ann Herzog

The life of Anne Hutchinson comes most dramatically into view between the years 1636 and 1638. It was during these two years that the leaders of the Massachusetts Bay Colony felt threatened first by the theological teachings and finally by the very presence of this remarkable woman. The picture of Anne Hutchinson's life blurs a great deal before and after these dramatic two years. It is clear that Anne Hutchinson stepped outside the boundaries acceptable for women in the 1600s, and much of the reaction against her must be understood in this context. She left no personal diary to give us a clear image, and therefore we must speculate in order to piece together the whole of her life.

During Anne Hutchinson's forty-three years in England she raised a large family and became inspired through the ministry of John Cotton. It was Cotton's move to New England that led to Hutchinson's decision to move her family to Boston so that she could remain near Cotton. As we will show, Hutchinson moved slowly away from a strict following of Cotton's teaching until she finally was brought to trial for her heterodox views. This trial resulted in her excommunication from the First Church of Boston and in her banishment from the Massachusetts Bay Colony. The last five years of Anne Hutchinson's life were spent in Rhode Island, then New York, where she was killed by Indians at the age of fifty-two.

We attempt here to account Anne Hutchinson's life and beliefs, looking at the early relationships that may have influenced her, as well as at the religious climate she grew up in. We shall attempt to understand the whole of her life and not to examine just the few years during which her actions were most controversial. In this way it is possible to trace the development of Anne Hutchinson's faith from her childhood in Alford, England, to her death in Westchester, New York. By reflecting on the images of Anne Hutchinson's faith and the impact of her faith on others, we may hope to understand more fully the struggles of contemporary women with religious establishments.

Childhood and Family

Anne Marbury was born in 1591, the daughter of Francis Marbury and his second wife Bridget Dryden Marbury. Francis Marbury's family was from Bain, England, and in 1584 he settled in Alford, about fifteen miles southeast of Bain. Alford is a small town located not far from the English coast and about one hundred miles north of Cambridge. The thatched-roof houses of Alford were built alongside the fords that gave the town its name. Bridget Marbury's family, the Drydens of Canons Ashby, lived in the neighboring county of Northamptonshire. Anne Marbury and the poet John Dryden were second cousins. Apart from Bridget's family background, and the fact that she bore fourteen children, we know nothing about her life. Francis' life, though, is known, and glimpses of it help place Anne's life in the context of family influences.

Both the Drydens and the Marburys were families of moderate wealth. A silver shield depicting the arms of the Marbury family has a border of semicircles, considered to be a sign of distinction. On the belt of the shield are three sheaves of grain in silver "an 'exceedingly ancient and honorable' device indicative of plenty and generosity."[1] In the case of Francis and Bridget Marbury, this distinguished heritage was to be carried on by their eldest daughter, Anne, and not their eldest son, John. The lineage of distinction seems to have passed from Francis to Anne and then, three generations later, to Thomas Hutchinson, the last royal governor of the Massachusetts Bay Colony.

Anne Marbury's father opposed the established clergy all his life. We have a record of one of his trials and a condensed version written by Marbury himself of his examination before the Lord Bishop of London.

Francis Marbury (*b.*1556) studied theology at Christ College, Cambridge and was ordained deacon in the Church of England. In the *Proceedings* of the Massachusetts Historical Society, Frederic L. Gay tells us:

> He became the deacon of a parish in the town of Northampton, and a license to preach was issued to him. He evidently fancied himself as a preacher, though he had barely attained manhood, and soon indulged in such unorthodox pronouncements, that he was hailed before the ecclesiastical court, and proving contumacious was committed to prison. After some time in dolorous and uncomfortable confinement he was released, but was distinctly forbidden to revisit the scene of his ministrations at Northampton. But being a Marbury, with the family characteristic of stubborn pride, he determined to disregard these unjustifiable directions, and was soon back again in the pulpit at Northampton, giving vent to pronounced views upon the failings of the clergy on which he held an opinion strengthened by his own mis-treatment.[2]

In 1578, Marbury, aged twenty-two, was back in prison, having "boldly accused the Lord Bishop himself of inadequacy."[3] He remained in confinement until the

63

bishop cooled down. We do not know how long this imprisonment lasted. It seems probable that he began a new ministry about 1582. We do know he married his first wife, Elizabeth Moore, in 1584 and settled with her in Alford. Around 1589 Francis Marbury was again brought to trial for his heterodoxy, and this trial ended his preaching career for fifteen years until, at age forty-nine, he resumed his ministry in the city of London.

Francis and Elizabeth had two daughters, Susan and Elizabeth. Elizabeth died while giving birth to their third child in 1587. Four years later Francis and Bridget Dryden were married. When Anne Marbury was born in 1591, she was the object of the curious attention of her two half-sisters, Susan, who was then six, Elizabeth, five, and her brother John, aged two.

Many relatives lived within walking distance, and Anne's early life was dominated by family relationships. Bridget was probably pleased to have her own daughter, and no doubt Anne felt wanted and loved. We know she loved her father very much and spent a great deal of time with him, especially during her early childhood. At this time, Francis had plenty of free time: no longer preaching, he signed "gentleman" after his name and nothing else. This indicates that there was no other occupation to fill his time when he was not serving as a minister.

Bridget and Francis Marbury's next child, Bridget, was born in 1593. Anne's first two years were spent without a younger rival for her parents' and siblings' attention. Bridget died at the age of five. Her death, when Anne was seven, probably made Anne acutely aware of the mortality of those she loved. The minister Francis Marbury, in the Calvinist tradition that shaped his theology, probably explained Bridget's death to Anne in terms of God's will, heightening her awareness of God. A boy was born the following year, in 1594, and life continued in Anne's family. Anne may have wondered, as children will, whether she had done something to cause Bridget's death. She may have felt even at the age of seven, as she certainly did later in life, a strong sense of responsibility for those around her.

We know it was possible for Anne during those early years to have a formal education unusual for girls of that day. Alford was one of the few towns to have a local grammar school with fellowships awarded to good students for further education at Cambridge University. A number of Anne's brothers did go on to Cambridge; that, however, was not considered for Anne. From the age of seven to age thirteen, Anne went to school, saw four younger brothers born, and, in 1599, the family welcomed a younger sister, also named Bridget.

The faith development theory leads us to hypothesize that the roots of Anne's adult faith took firm hold in the household of the gentleman–dissenting preacher of Alford. From her birth until the birth of her younger sister, Bridget, Anne's faith would have been prelingual and preconceptual. She would have formed a sense of the world and her place in it on the basis of her experiences of care and relationship, primarily in the home. From Bridget's birth until her death, when Anne was seven, we expect that Anne's alert and imaginative mind responded resonantly to the talk, the actions of worship and compassion, and the other visible signs of faith in her parents. We can be sure, as well, that her intuitive-projective imagination gave her powerful experiences of the uncanny, the mysterious, the fanciful, the magical. Around the time of Bridget's death and Anne's starting to school, we would expect Anne to experience a transition toward mythic-literal faith. Here she gradually separated beliefs and ritual actions found acceptable in the Christian community from those fanciful, unsanctioned products of her imagination. She began to learn the language of her father's faith and undoubtedly began to shape a child's

fierce loyalty to the familial commitments whose impera-
tives—and those to which they were opposed—she began
dimly to grasp.

Leaving Alford and Childhood

In 1604 when Anne was thirteen, Francis Marbury was
called to Saint Martin's Vintry in London, and the family
left the home of Anne's childhood.

The move to London probably increased Anne's sense
of identification with her family even as she encountered
many new sorts and conditions of people. The beliefs of
her father and of the community of Alford gave Anne a
sense of belonging to a group and gave her a window
through which to see the rest of the world. Anne was an
outsider in this new setting; yet she probably remained
secure. She had been provided a firm set of norms and
beliefs from which she created a cohesive worldview based
in large part on her father's teachings. These teachings will
reappear later in Anne's life: she, like her father, was on
the way to being a theological radical.

But for Anne, in contrast to most of her contemporaries,
the theological radicalism of her father and his household
was experienced by her as *conventional,* that is, as a part of
the taken-for-granted wisdom. She imbibed it with her
nourishment and through the family's everyday routines.
This radical theological content, which was to make up the
substance of Anne's synthetic-conventional faith for
nearly two decades, would not be truly radical until it
became a matter of her own autonomous, adult recompo-
sition and commitment.

The family lived in the rectory of Saint Martin's Vintry
in these years, and Anne grew to adulthood in London.
She had a constant home, and it probably was during this
period that Anne learned midwifery. So far as we know,
her formal schooling ended when she left Alford. In 1611,

six months before Anne's twenty-first birthday, Francis Marbury—her father, minister, and teacher—died. We have no record of Anne's relationship with her mother; her attachment to her father can be deduced by how closely she later duplicated—possibly attempted to live out—his life through her theological ideas and her temperament. Anne did not publicly mourn her father very long. On August 9, 1612, a few weeks before her birthday, she married William Hutchinson.

Wife, Midwife and Mystic

William Hutchinson was from Alford, and apparently he went to London to persuade Anne to marry him. His father had been mayor of Alford for a brief time, and the men of his family were principally merchants dealing in cloth. William carried on his family's tradition and was known to be sturdy and dependable. Different from Anne's father in many ways, William upheld customs and traditions and did not raise stormy issues as Francis had done.

Anne and William returned to Alford, where they lived for the next twenty years and where Anne bore eight children in the first ten years—fourteen altogether while living in Alford. Although we have little record of Anne and William's married life in Alford, we do know that they often made the trip to Boston, in Lincolnshire, to hear John Cotton preach from the pulpit of St. Botolph's Church.

The trip, a distance of twenty-four miles, must have taken close to eight hours each way. When Cotton became vicar of St. Botolph's Church in 1612, at the age of twenty-seven, he had conformed to the Church of England. After about three years he became a Nonconformist and soon was well known for his Nonconformist beliefs and his powerful sermons. The so-called Middle

Way in which Cotton believed appealed strongly to Anne Hutchinson. This was the middle way between English Separatism and the presbyterian form of church government. Cotton did not advocate a total break from the Church of England but felt that many reforms were crucial.

Separatism had been growing in England, especially since 1581, when Robert Harrison had formed an independent congregation. Separatists and Nonconformists were often imprisoned, expelled from England, or hanged. Charles I (1625–1649) was as unpopular with the reformers as his father James I had been; this unpopularity resulted in the large Puritan exodus to America. Cotton became part of this exodus in 1633. By that time Anne Hutchinson had become one of his devoted followers and was moving toward close spiritual identification with him.

Cotton stood in the same tradition of critical tension with the Church of England as had Francis Marbury. In Cotton, Anne Hutchinson's nurture in the conventions of dissenting ecclesiology found support and extension. The frequent trips Anne and William made to hear Cotton preach are evidence that the Hutchinsons' household was largely shaped in accordance with Anne's faith heritage. Their gravitation toward Cotton really required no serious break with the past but was more a matter of continuity.

During the early years of married life in Alford, Anne learned about herbs for healing the sick and practiced midwifery; she began to be identified as a healer.[4] It was not until her late thirties that Anne again experienced change—a change that foreshadowed some of the most momentous times of her life. It was during a time of mental and spiritual unrest that Anne underwent a religious experience of revelation and turmoil. She struggled with herself as she experienced God and the importance of theological ideas in a personal way. She felt that she heard the word of God, and that what she heard was clearly contrary to the teachings of the Church of England. No longer was she satisfied to listen to others and ponder their ideas: she needed direct experience to know what was right for her. Years later she said:

> Being much troubled to see the falseness of the constitution of the church of England, I like to have turned separatist; whereupon I kept a day of solemn humiliation and pondering of the thing: this scripture was brought unto me—he that denies Jesus Christ to be come in the flesh is antichrist . . . I bless the Lord, he hath let me see which was the clear ministry and which the wrong. Since that time I confess I have been more choice and he hath let me to distinguish between the voice of my beloved and the voice of Moses, the voice of John Baptist and the voice of antichrist, for all those voices are spoken of in scripture.[5]

A biographer describes the day of Anne Hutchinson's initial revelation without citing any sources. The description may not, however, be too far removed from fact:

> In agony of mind and spirit Anne kept a day of solemn humiliation in the hope of coming to a decision. . . . The master ate his meal hastily and departed as from a house of mourning. . . . Still Anne wrestled with her problem. Without food and without rest, behind her closed door she sought guidance from her Bible. . . . [Finally] the mistress descended from her chamber and the house smiled again.[6]

New World View, New World

Whatever actually happened that day, we can be sure that Anne Hutchinson's faith commitment no longer rested solely on the conventional nurture she had received in her childhood and adolescent home. A mature woman, mother, midwife, she had now undergone an experience of intense wrestling and spiritual breakthroughs in which the authority of God's word in scripture has been etched on her own heart. Never again would the mediation of divine authority through ecclesial spokespersons be the final recourse for Anne. Her new standing place, informed by individuative-reflective faith, placed her in uncharted and dangerous terrain for a sixteenth-century woman.

Cotton and the Separatist community became Hutchinson's focus in a new way. This influence was so profound that when Cotton moved to the Massachusetts Bay Colony, Anne Hutchinson was left desolate. John Winthrop wrote in his *Short Story of the Rise, Reign, and Ruine of the Antinomians, Familists, and Libertines* quoting Anne Hutchinson's feelings about Cotton:

> Then it pleased God to reveal himself to me in that of Esay 30.20 Though the Lord give thee the Bread of adversity, & c. yet thine eyes shall see thy teachers; after this the Lord carrying Mr. Cotton to New England (at which I was much troubled) it was revealed to me, that I must go thither also, and that there I would be persecuted and suffer much trouble. . . . Though I must come to New England, yet I must not feare nor be dismayed.[7]

In 1634, at the age of forty-three, Anne Hutchinson sailed with her family on the *Griffin* to the Massachusetts Bay Colony. We can imagine what that move must have meant to them. We have a sense of Anne Hutchinson's strength in her persuading her family to move to the "New Land" at this early stage of its development. The Hutchinsons left their secure, stable existence in Alford to follow Anne's mentor and spiritual teacher. William gave up his prospering business, and they left friends and relatives. It is important to note her age at the time of the move. This was no young, idealistic woman, but an experienced wife, mother, and midwife. Her move to the New World began a new stage in her life. She was still wife, mother, and midwife; now she was to be also a theologian.

It was on the voyage that Anne made her first enemy in the colony. Reverend Zachariah Symmes preached incessantly on the journey, and Anne reportedly had many theological discussions with him. Symmes vented his anger against her immediately upon arrival, reporting her supposed heresies. William Hutchinson was admitted to the church membership on October 26, 1634, shortly after their arrival; Anne's admission to the church was delayed until November 2 because of Symmes' warnings.

Anne had another early enemy, Mr. William Bartholomew. In London Bartholomew and Anne had walked together through St. Paul's Churchyard, and he remembered their conversation: "She became very inquisitive after revelations and said that she had never had any great thing done about her but it was revealed before hand."[8]

Thus she arrived in the Massachusetts Bay Colony in the company of two prominent colonists who had become extremely wary of her beliefs and her habit of expressing them.

Anne's first two years in the colony were spent settling in and getting used to the new life. A house was built, warm clothes made, and new neighbors met. She also practiced midwifery and attended to her neighbors' illnesses.

> At her first coming she was well respected and esteemed of me not only because herself and her family were well beloved in England at Alford in Lincolnshire; not only because she with her family came over hither (as was said) for conscience' sake: but chiefly that I heard she did much good in our Town, women's meetings, childbirth travails, good discourse about their spiritual estates.[9]

John Cotton remained ambivalent about his relationship with Anne and in his support of her. He finally, at her examination by the General Court in Newtowne, made clear that he did not support all her beliefs, and that he and she distinctly did not believe the same doctrines. It is from this that we know Anne Hutchinson's theological positions must have changed during the time between her arrival in Boston and this examination three years later. She had come to New England to be near her "teacher," John Cotton; but they rarely spoke, and her beliefs grew in a different direction from his. Cotton vacillated between supporting her and disagreeing with her; she never knew, until the time of her examination, whether she had an ally in Cotton.

Mistress Hutchinson's Meetings

The women's meetings Cotton mentions were heatedly discussed by the members of the colony, especially during the years 1635–1638. The men had long been used to gathering after religious meetings to discuss the contents of the sermon. With Anne's arrival the women also began to gather. In 1635 John Wilson, the regular minister of First Church, Boston, left for England to settle some family matters. During his absence, John Cotton filled the pulpit; for a year Cotton was the sole minister to the community. In this capacity as minister to the colony, Cotton visited Anne, probably in the summer of 1635, to discuss her "spiritual condition." It was this discussion that sharpened the controversy.

When Anne was asked why meetings were held at her house she replied:

It is lawful for me so to do, as it is all our practices and can you find a warrant for yourself and condemn me for the same things? The ground of my taking it up when I first came to this land was because I did not go to such meetings as those were, it was presently reported that I did not allow of such meetings but held them unlawful and therefore in that regard they said I was proud and did despise all ordinances, upon that friend came unto me and told me of it and I to prevent such aspersions took it up but it was in practice before I came, therefore I was not the first.[10]

Cotton was the friend Anne Hutchinson refers to, and he was not pleased at the form her faith took: "He professed himself puzzled and dismayed that her faith seemed to have its source and strength, not from the public ministry but only from her own private meditations."[11] Anne had agreed to meet with the women of the community; and thus began the weekly meetings in the Hutchinson home, ostensibly to discuss the sermon of the week before. At first, Anne did keep to the subject of Cotton's sermon; she would then go on, however, to analyze, criticize, and discuss the sermon in such a way as to communicate her own ideas. By the spring of 1635 these meetings were sometimes drawing between eighty and a hundred women; a second weekly meeting was added to include both women and men.

The influential members of the community were involved in these meetings. They included William Coddington, the wealthiest man in the colony; William Brenton and Robert Harding, prosperous merchants; Hutchinson relatives; Mary and William Dyer, and many others. "Her roster revealed some significant absentees, most notably Winthrop and Bellingham, but otherwise she could count among her adherents almost all Bostonians who were regularly elected to high public office."[12]

There are two important problems concerning the meetings in Anne Hutchinson's home. The first concerns the issues that Anne was raising and the corollary that she presumed not only to disagree with accepted theological authority, but flatly categorized the prevailing ideas as incorrect. The second issue is perhaps more pervasive and subtle. Anne Hutchinson spoke with confidence and strength. In her courageous embodiment of individuative-reflective faith, she was a woman who stepped outside rigidly defined sex roles and attracted many other women of the community to her. In trying to understand what Anne's followers found so attractive, it is important to think not only of the articulated theories but of the assumptions and behaviors of the colony as well. The two points are not entirely separate. The bridge between them has to do with what Anne Hutchinson called "the covenant of grace."

Anne Hutchinson felt that personal experience of God was possible for everyone, and that it was only through revelations and knowledge of the Spirit that one was saved. She said that John Wilson and most of the other ministers in the area preached a "Covenant of Works," which required one to live by a series of laws that supposedly defined the moral life.[13] "And the difficulty with that was that many of those recognized as Christians by these Godly evidences, had no grace in their hearts at all."[14] Hutchinson called the ministers "legalists" and said they were not qualified to judge whether one experienced God's grace. She argued that sanctification, or the living out of the moral life as preached by the clergy, was not necessarily a sign of either justification or the inward knowledge of God's grace. Hutchinson told her followers not to have confidence that their "works" would save them but to search for God and pray for personal knowledge of the Light. She objected to the ministers allowing people to "thinke [themselves] to be saved, because they see some worke of Sanctification in them."[15] Anne said that one should look for Christ and not for promises, sanctification, and graces.[16] Here we see the pietistic element in her theology. Personal faith and the search for God in prayer were the most important things to her; unlike her antagonists, who felt that duties or works were signs or, as some thought, the necessary preparations for grace. What counted for Anne was experience.

The Covenant of Grace is very close to what I. M. Lewis, the noted English anthropologist, calls Spirit Theology, which speaks particularly to women. Lewis describes the tension between main-morality religion, here represented by Wilson and the other Bay Colony clergy, and peripheral religion, which is often a type of protest by the oppressed members of society, usually women.[17] Peripheral religion can also be understood as the shadow side of the often patriarchal main-morality religion.

When the peripheral religion becomes too successful, the powerful leaders of main-morality religion try to restore order, often accusing the leader of the peripheral religion of witchcraft. Lewis points to a cross-cultural history of the connection between witchcraft and peripheral religion. The three major controversies of the seventeenth century in the Massachusetts Bay Colony (Anne Hutchinson in 1636, the Quaker persecutions of the late 1650s, and the witchcraft hysteria of 1692) were all attempts by the people of the Bay to "clarify their position in the world as a whole, to redefine the boundaries which set New England apart as a new experiment in living."[18]

In all three episodes it was women who were pushing hardest against the boundaries; indeed, these three struggles can be seen as struggles between male authority and powerless women. In the 1630s there were only whisperings about witchcraft in the Massachusetts Bay Colony. Most of this undercurrent of witchcraft talk was about Anne Hutchinson, providing for the men in the colony a way to make sense of this remarkable woman who defied traditional female behavioral boundaries.

It is not surprising that Anne Hutchinson's ideas of the Covenant of Grace would attract so many women and become cultlike. We have only to look at the life of the Puritan woman to see many of the underlying problems.

Anne Hutchinson was reacting not only to specific theological ideas, but to the norms and unwritten laws of the day, not the least of which concerned a woman's "place."

> That Anne Hutchinson and many other Puritan women should at stressful times rebel, either by explicit statement or by implicit example, against the role they were expected to fulfill in society is readily understandable, since that role, in both old and New England, was extremely limiting. The model English woman was weak, submissive, charitable, virtuous and modest. Her mental and physical activity was limited to keeping the home in order, cooking, and bearing and rearing children, although she might occasionally serve the community as a nurse or midwife. She was urged to avoid books and intellectual exercise, for such activity might overtax her weak mind, and to serve her husband willingly, since she was by nature his inferior.[19]

Controversy and Confrontation

Anne Hutchinson vocalized what many others, including some men, felt. Men were certainly included in the ranks of what has been called the "Hutchinsonian movement." Our discussion here emphasizes the involvement of the women in the community because it was so unusual for women to meet publicly as a group and express ideas. John Winthrop records typical male reaction to women who had ideas: "Ann Hopkins, wife of the Governor of Connecticut, had lost her understanding and reason by giving herself solely to reading and writing."[20] The women who attended the meetings in Anne Hutchinson's home were expressing themselves in a radical and rebellious way, and when this became too threatening to the standard-bearers of the status quo, a meeting was called by John Cotton to try to smooth things over.

Cotton called his gathering when it became clear to him that Anne was not espousing his beliefs in her weekly meetings, and when Anne's disagreements with all the ministers of the area became public. She excluded her brother-in-law John Wheelwright—and usually John Cotton—from her criticism; nevertheless, Cotton felt uneasy because it was known that the Hutchinsons had come to the colony because of him. Thus Cotton invited many of the area ministers, including Hugh Peters from Salem, Zachariah Symmes of Charlestown, Thomas Shepherd of Newtowne, Weld of Roxbury, Phillips of Watertown, Ward of Ipswich, John Wilson, and John Wheelwright, to come for a meeting. And Cotton invited Anne Hutchinson.

The meeting did not proceed as Cotton had hoped it would, and the ministers left more opposed to Anne Hutchinson than they had been previously. Weld of Roxbury stayed behind, and he and Anne had a conversation that Weld later denied during Anne's examination by the General Court. During this examination John Winthrop, then Governor, asked Thomas Leverett, a ruling elder of the Boston Church, "Don't you remember that she said they were not able ministers of the New Testament?" Anne answered Winthrop's question and said:

> Mrs. H.: Mr. Weld and I had an hour's discourse at the window and then I spake that, if I spake it.[21]

What followed must have left Anne feeling betrayed. Here started a pattern of private conversation used in public to condemn her. Weld responded to Anne's statement, saying:

> Mr. Weld: Will you affirm that in the court? Did not I say unto you, Mrs. Hutchinson, before the elders? When I

produced the thing, you then called for proof. Was not my answer to you, leave it there, and if I cannot prove it you shall be blameless?

Mrs. H.: This I remember I spake, but do you not remember that I came afterwards to the window when you was writing and there spake unto you?

Mr. Weld: No truly.

Mrs. H.: But I do very well.

Gov. Winthrop: Mr. Cotton, the court desires that you declare what you do remember of the conference which was at the time and is now in question.

Mr. Cotton: I did not think I should be called to bear witness in this cause and therefore did not labour to call to remembrance what was done. . . .[22]

Cotton's statement that he "did not labour to call to remembrance what was done" finally made clear that he would not support Anne. In 1648 Cotton wrote *The Way of Congregational Churches Cleared,* in which he said:

I must needs profess, that cannot be made good by any witness of truth, Mistris Hutchinson seldome resorted to me: and when she did, she did seldome or never (that I can tell of) that she tarried long, I rather think, she was loath to resort much to me, or to conferre long with me, lest she might seeme to learne somewhat from me. And withall I know (by good proof) she was very careful to prevent any jealousie in mee, that shee should harbour any private opinions, differing from the course of my publick Ministry which she could not well have avoided, if she kept almost every day so private and long discourse with mee.[23]

Clearly Cotton was no longer the important figure in Anne's life that he had been in England. It may be surmised that her success among the members of the community may have encouraged her and enabled her to move toward a more autonomous expression of her faith. Clearly she felt a need to express her views and to be active in persuading others of their merits. The most important thing in Anne's life had become the expression of her faith.

It is believed that Anne went to the meeting at Cotton's house thinking that the ministers were truly interested in her beliefs and wished to be more clearly informed of them. Instead, that meeting led to most of the charges later brought against her at her examination.

Anne Hutchinson was deeply embroiled with her opponents in what became known as the Antinomian Controversy. A grasp of the issues involved is quite difficult for two reasons. The first has to do with the motive, often only partially conscious, that focused on sex-role behavior and Anne's leadership qualities, which attracted many women and men in the community. The second reason has to do with the complexity of the theological issues involved. As was mentioned, we can describe the conflict between a Covenant of Grace and a Covenant of Works; however, as Kai Erikson has accurately pointed out, the controversy "was often a confusing affair even to its most active participants."[24] John Winthrop, and sixty years later Cotton Mather, said few people understood the issues. Mather wrote: "Tis believed that multitudes of persons, who took in with both parties, did never to their dying day understand what the difference was."[25] Erikson attributes this conflict to a shift of boundaries, articulated by conflict. As a possible underlying structure, we are pointing to boundary shifts as well as to the success of the peripheral religion focused on the Spirit, or the Covenant of Grace, to which women historically have turned for self-expression.

The term "Antinomian" was one of derision dating to John Agricola, a follower of Luther. "In the widest sense the term is used to designate the doctrines of extreme fanatics who deny subjection to any law other than the subjective caprices of the empirical individual."[26] When this term is applied to the Hutchinson movement it describes a conflict that aroused to great fervor the oppressed and the oppressors. In this new world there probably was a feeling that whatever happened would be new, important, and tradition-making. The American Puritan heritage was being formed, challenged and cemented at this time.

The Politics of Patriarchy

During 1636 and 1637 Anne became increasingly involved in the politics of the colony. Anne knew that it was impossible for her to become a teacher in the First Church of Boston, and so she persuaded her brother-in-law and friend, Wheelwright, to take this position. The plan backfired; and Wheelwright, after delivering a fast-day sermon, was convicted of sedition. The same day Wheelwright was convicted, it was decided that new elections would be held in Newtowne, in what is today Cambridge, rather than in Boston, where Anne had most of her supporters; she had no supporters in Newtowne. Henry Vane, Anne's good friend and supporter, was governor at this time; but the May elections threatened to change that. The two months between the March decision to have the elections and the May elections saw Hutchinson's supporters busily trying to convince as many as they could that Vane should be reelected and Wheelwright cleared. When Vane called the election to order he announced the first order of business was to take action on the petition from Boston on behalf of Wheelwright. This caused Winthrop to object that it was out of order, and finally Vane had to concede, put it aside, and hold the election.

The results of the election were disastrous to Anne Hutchinson. John Winthrop, one of Anne's most vocal antagonists, was elected governor; and Thomas Dudley was elected deputy governor. Both Winthrop and Dudley took active roles against Anne during both her examination and trial. The three magistrates who were Anne's supporters—Vane, Coddington, and Hough—were dropped from the magistracy, and John Endicott was made a magistrate for life. Endicott, along with Winthrop and Dudley, was antagonistic to Hutchinson. The plan to have the election in Newtowne instead of Boston worked. Vane returned to England in August of that year, and one of the first acts of the new government was to call a synod on August 30, 1637, to clear up the case of Anne Hutchinson, dispense with the case of John Wheelwright, and discover John Cotton's connection with the entire controversy.

The synod, also called the First Council of the Congregational Churches in America, lasted three weeks, during which time eighty-two opinions of the blasphemies of the Hutchinsonian movement were discussed. The meeting was open to the public; but, because Anne Hutchinson was a woman, she was not allowed to speak to defend herself. At the conclusion of the synod, the men present decreed that Wheelwright be banished from the colony within two weeks' time and that Anne Hutchinson be called before the General Court to answer the charges placed against her.

The examination of Anne Hutchinson took place in Newtowne at what is today the corner of Dunster and Mt. Auburn Streets in Cambridge. It is thought that the reason the examination was held in Newtowne rather than in Boston was to make it difficult for Anne's supporters to attend. The General Court convened in November of 1637, and we have a full account of both her examination and the later trial.

The examination lasted for two wearying days. Anne, required to stand, faced Winthrop and her other adversaries arguing theology. She could not argue her sex.

At the beginning of the examination Anne and Winthrop bantered back and forth; Anne trying to force

Winthrop to say specifically what law she had transgressed, and Winthrop finally saying Anne had broken a commandment by dishonoring parents. In this case he said the fathers of the commonwealth were the parents Anne dishonored. Finally he seems to have grown frustrated: "We do not mean to discourse with those of your sex but only this; you do adhere unto them and do endeavour to set forward this faction and so you do dishonour us."[27] The discussion then focused on the meetings in Anne's home. Anne referred to Titus 2: 3, 4, and 5, saying there is a clear rule "that the elder women should instruct the younger."[28] Winthrop seemed very upset that Anne might also teach men; he was also upset that she taught younger women wrongly: "You must take it [I Cor. 14:34-35] in this sense that elder women must instruct the younger about their business, and to love their husband and not to make them clash."[29] Arguments continued about the Covenant of Works, and many ministers spoke against Anne, some vehemently.

Finally they broke for the night, and the next morning Anne asked that the witnesses speak under oath. This caused a flurry of reaction; the accusers thought themselves insulted, and finally Hugh Peters said that the "oath is not to satisfy Mrs. Hutchinson but the court."[30] There was much fumbling in the attempt to ensnare Anne Hutchinson. The mood seems to have changed when Anne described her period of spiritual change in England. She was challenged by a Mr. Nowell, who asked: "How did you know that that was the Spirit?" Anne replied, "How did Abraham know it was God that bid him offer his son, being a breach of the sixth commandment?" Deputy Governor Dudley answered, saying "by an immediate voice"; and Anne said, "So to me by an immediate revelation. . . . Ever since that time I have been confident of what he hath revealed to me."[31] Anne's old enemy Bartholomew warned the court "that her revelations will deceive," and the court listened intently to Bartholomew's words.[32]

Anne Hutchinson's biographers surmise that the court might have been satisfied with merely censuring her until she began to talk about her revelations. Cotton would not in any way support her once she began speaking of them and finally made this clear in response to a question by Mr. Dudley: "But if it be in the way of miracle or a revelation without the word that I do not assent to, but look at it as a delusion, and I think so doth she too as I understand her."[33] The result of the two-day-long examination, most of which Anne had to endure on her feet, was pronounced by John Winthrop: "Mrs. Hutchinson, the sentence of the court you hear is that you are banished from out of our jurisdiction as being a woman not fit for our society, and are to be imprisoned till the court shall send you away."[34] Hearing this, Anne turned to John Winthrop and said, "I desire to know wherefore I am banished?" Winthrop replied, "Say no more, the court knows wherefore and is satisfied."[35]

The court could not tolerate Anne's belief in her direct communication with the Spirit. We have only a hint of what went on in the minds and hearts of those who banished Anne; however, we do get a sense of the fear they felt. The words of this woman could no longer be tolerated by the men of the colony.

We can see here the undercurrent themes of sex-role violation and the fear of claims to direct revelation that many ministers had. As long as Anne restricted herself to midwifery and the care of the sick, we have what Lewis describes as "a feminist sub-culture, with an ecstatic religion restricted to women and protected from male attack through its representation as a therapy for illness."[36] When Anne's healing and wisdom became more public and she began to "minister" to women and men, she was no longer protected from male attack. She attempted to create a comprehensive theology out of this subculture or peripheral religion, and this pushed the boundaries too far to be tolerated. The attack was so confusing to all for two reasons: first, because of the nature of conflicts between peripheral religion and main-morality religion, and second, because Anne Hutchinson's outspoken embodiment of a radical individuative-reflective faith threatened the male-dominated synthetic-conventional society to its very roots.

Expression of faith by women was tolerated as long as it was confined to the rules of the male hierarchy. When the women of the Massachusetts Bay Colony broke out of their traditional roles by following a woman leader, a great deal of fear and panic resulted. The differences of women—their unknown qualities and behavior and their mysterious bodies—were contained and made less frightening by the complex conventional social system with its mores and taboos. In the midst of this crisis all the conventional beliefs and mores were shaken. This peripheral stage 4 religious impulse had to be contained—even if the rules for containment were made up as they went along.

Trial and Banishment

Anne was forced to spend the winter in the home of Joseph Weld, the brother of the man who denied conversing with her at Cotton's house. She was forced to endure constant visits by ministers, each wishing to discuss her heresies with her and to be the one to make her see the error of her ways. Finally in March of 1638 Anne Hutchinson was brought to trial by the First Church of Boston, and John Wilson had the opportunity to denounce Anne publicly.

By the time of the trial, Anne's husband and most of their children, along with many friends, had left for the south to find a new home in Rhode Island. Only her son

Richard and her son-in-law Thomas Savage were present to support Anne.

The results of the conversations during the winter at Weld's home were used as new evidence in the trial. As the ministers read one error after another, only Richard and Thomas gave vocal support. Finally they were both silenced, and there was agreement among the whole church, "and so they proceeded to Admonition."[37]

John Cotton addressed the women of the congregation, and then all the women generally:

Many of you I fear have bine too much seduced and led aside by her, therefore *I admonish you* in the lord to looke to yourselves and to take heed that you receive nothinge for Truth which hath not the stamp of the Word of God from it. . . . Let me say this to you all, and to all the Sisters of other Congregations. Let not the good you have receved from her, make you receve all for good that comes from her for you see she is but a Woman and many unsound and dayngerous principles are held by her. . . .[38]

Anne tried to acknowledge some mistakes, but this seems to have further infuriated her judges. Finally John Wilson said, "The Church consenting to it we will proceed to Excommunication."

Forasmuch as you, Mrs. Hutchinson, have highly transgressed and offended and forasmuch as you have soe many times *troubled the Church with your Erors* and have drawen away many a poor soule and have *upheld you Revelations;* and forasmuch as *you have made a Lye,* etc. Therefor in the name of our Lord Jesus Christ and in the name of the Church I doe not only pronounce you worthy to be cast out, but *I doe cast you out* and in the name of Christ *I doe* deliver you up to Sathan that you may learne no more to blaspheme to seduce and to lye. And I doe account you from this time forth to be a Heathen and a Publican and soe to be held of all the

Brethren and Sisters of this Congregation, and of others. Therefor *I command you* in the name of Christ Jesus and of this Church *as a Leper to withdraw yourselfe out of the Congregation:* that as formerly you have dispised and comtemned the Holy Ordinances of God and turned your Backe one them, soe you may now have no part in them nor benefit by them.[39]

Anne Hutchinson's last public words in Boston were spoken as she walked out of the church after hearing the searing excommunication. In response to someone who remarked "the Lord sanctify this unto you," she said: "The Lord judgeth not as man judgeth. Better to be cast out of the church than to deny Christ." Mary Dyer, later hanged by some of these same men for her Quaker beliefs, stood up and walked out of the church with her friend Anne Hutchinson.

Exile

Anne Hutchinson's faith development did not stop here. Anne continued to grow and change until her death. The Antinomian Controversy was certainly a major part of this development, and the heated nature of it fits the social milieu as well as Anne's individual faith stage.

On March 28, 1638, Anne Hutchinson left for Rhode Island, where William had been preparing a home. It is reported that in July or August of that year Anne had a hydatidiform mole, a type of miscarriage, and John Winthrop reports in his *Short Story:* "And see how the wisdome of God fitted this judgement to her sinne every way, for looke as she had vented mishapen opinions, so she must bring forth deformed monsters."[40]

We have very few documents describing the years of Anne's life after she left Boston. As in her first forty-three years, we have hints at what her life was like and must conjecture from the pieces about the whole.

She settled in Portsmouth, Rhode Island, and, with her friend Coddington, led the small community spiritually and politically. "Here Anne resumed the position she had held in Boston society before her catastrophe. She was surrounded by a tiny court of friends and kinsmen. She was a preacher; perhaps, for a while, she was THE preacher."[41] Anne was moving more and more toward a preference for a society free of magistrates. Not long after settling in, the three magistrates were removed, and William Hutchinson was elected sole magistrate. It is reported that "Mrs. Hutchinson persuaded her husband to resign his position after one year because of the opinion, which newly she had taken up, of the unlawfulness of magistry."[42]

The Boston Church continued to keep an ear to the happenings of the Rhode Island community and apparently sent a committee to reason with them, hoping they would stop associating with Anne Hutchinson. Wilson sent a warning to Rhode Island to have no communication with Anne Hutchinson on peril of penalties like her own.[43] It is unclear what Wilson had in mind, since he had no jurisdiction over the people in Rhode Island; clearly, however, Anne Hutchinson and her followers still were felt to be a threat. A committee of three was sent to investigate the situation in Rhode Island: Edward Gibbon, William Gibbon, and John Oliver. These men asked many what they thought of Anne Hutchinson, and when they asked William Hutchinson he said what constitutes his only recorded words: "I am more nearly tied to my wife than to the church. She is a deare Saint and a servant of God."[44] "The members of the above committee were refused permission to address the congregation of the church at Portsmouth in which Anne was dominant."[45] On March 16, 1640, the three men reported to the congregation in

Boston what William Hutchinson had said. They also reported a meeting with Anne Hutchinson, during which she did little more than usher them out.

Early in 1642, William Hutchinson became ill and died. In August of that year Anne moved to New York with her children Francis; Mary; Katherine; Anne and her husband, William Collins; Susanna; and the youngest, Zuryell, then six. Zuryell was Anne Hutchinson's only child to have been born in Boston, just a year after she arrived. Of Anne's other children, Richard was in London; and Faith and her husband, Thomas Savage, remained in Boston, as did Edward, who was the great-grandfather of Thomas Hutchinson. Bridget, Samuel, and Edward remained in Rhode Island. We know that the Hutchinson party probably first landed in Long Island, but made their home in Westchester, in the present town of Eastchester.

The peace Anne may have felt for the first time lasted only one year. On August 20, 1643, Anne and five of her children were killed by Indians in revenge for the Dutch policies toward them. Susanna, the only survivor, was taken hostage and returned by the Indians on September 12, 1657.

During that one year in New York significant changes occurred in Anne Hutchinson's life. For the first time she was no longer in the middle of political or theological controversies. Her isolated tract of land must have given her a great deal of solitude and quiet. Her husband dead, some of the older children married, Anne Hutchinson chose to move away from all friends and adult relatives and settle a fair distance from them. There is a sense of seclusion about this last move—a sense that she no longer wished to preach (for there was no church or community to preach to) and that she no longer wished to be involved in the political battles of her day. Anne Hutchinson withdrew for the first time in her life. There is no record that she traveled to women about to give birth, nor did she even settle close to another person. The closest neighbor was John Throckmorton, probably no nearer than a mile from Anne's house. This was quite a change for Anne. All her life she had lived in towns or cities. From Alford to London, Boston to Portsmouth, there were always neighbors within calling range.

We have no documentation of Anne Hutchinson's thoughts and beliefs during this time; however, we can hypothesize that Anne's faith changed. There was no longer a need to relate to a large community and affirm her faith through them. There was no longer a need to assert her beliefs. We do know that she welcomed Indians into her home with kindness and that she was settling into a new, more peaceful way of life.

Anne Hutchinson was entering a new stage of faith at the time of her death, a stage that was profoundly different from that of the late 1630s, when there was constant turmoil, battle, and controversy. For the first time, the external tensions were gone, and Anne moved into a more accepting, though more withdrawing, time of her life. The healing she did during the last year of her life was an internal healing. Anne turned from caring for everyone about her to caring for herself. It was in the last year of her life that Anne may have made a transition to paradoxical-consolidative faith, stage 5. Anne took full responsibility for herself and knew that no community or person could bring her completion. There was a letting go that was at the same time an acceptance of others. She let others be in a way she (and they) had not found possible before.

Bibliography

Abbott, Willis J. *Women of History*. Philadelphia: The John C. Winston Co., 1913.

Adams, Charles Francis, ed. *Antinomianism in the Colony of*

Massachusetts Bay, 1636–1638. New York: Publication of the Prince Society, 1894.

Augur, Helen. *An American Jezebel.* New York: Brentano's, 1930.

Battis, Emory. *Saints and Sectaries.* Chapel Hill: The University of North Carolina Press, 1962.

Bolton, Reginald Pelham, *A Woman Misunderstood: Anne, Wife of William Hutchinson.* New York: The Westchester County Historical Society, 1931.

Brooks, Geraldine. *Dames and Daughters of Colonial Days.* New York: Thomas Y. Crowell, 1900.

Curtis, Edith. *Anne Hutchinson, A Biography.* Cambridge: Washburn & Thomas, 1930.

Ehrenreich, Barbara and English Diedre. *Witches, Midwives, and Nurses, A History of Women Healers.* Old Westbury, N.Y.: The Feminist Press, 1973.

Ellis, George E. *Life of Anne Hutchinson.* In the Library of American Biography conducted by Jared Sparks. Boston: Charles C. Little and James Brown, 1847.

Emerson, Everett. *John Cotton.* New York: Twayne Publishers, 1965.

Erikson, Kai T. *Wayward Puritans, A Study in the Sociology of Deviance.* New York: John Wiley & Sons, 1966.

Hall, David D. *The Antinomian Controversy 1636–1638: A Documentary History.* Middletown, Conn.: Wesleyan University Press, 1968.

Hubbard, Elbert. *Little Journeys to the Homes of Great Reformers. Anne Hutchinson.* East Aurora, N.Y.: The Roycrofters, 1907.

Hufeland, J. *Anne Hutchinson and Other Papers.* White Plains, N.Y.: Westchester County Historical Society, 1929.

Hutchinson, Thomas. *The History of the Colony and Province of Massachusetts Bay,* ed. Lawrence Shaw Mayo. Cambridge: Harvard University Press, 1936.

Kenyon, Theda. *Scarlet Anne.* New York: Doubleday, Doran & Company, 1939.

Koehler, Lyle. "The Case of the American Jezebels: Anne Hutchinson and Female Agitation during the Years of Antinomian Turmoil 1636–1638." *The William and Mary Quarterly,* Vol. xxx, No. 1 (January 1974).

ANNE HUTCHINSON

Lewis, I. M. *Ecstatic Religion.* Middlesex, England: Penguin Books, 1971.

Miller, Perry. *The New England Mind: The 17th Century.* Boston. Beacon Press, 1939.

Rugg, Winifred King. *Unafraid: A Life of Anne Hutchinson.* Boston: Beacon Press, 1930. Reprinted by Books for Libraries Press, Freeport, New York, 1970.

Sickels, Eleanor. *In Calico and Crinoline.* New York: The Viking Press, 1935.

Stearns, Raymond. *The Strenuous Puritan, Hugh Peter.* Urbana: University of Illinois Press, 1954.

The Encyclopedia of Religion and Ethics, vol. 1. New York: Charles Scribner's Sons, 1908.

The History of New England from 1630–1649, vol. 1. Boston: Little Brown and Company, 1880.

The Massachusetts Historical Society Proceedings and Collections.

Wheelwright, John. *His Writings Including His Fast Day Sermon, His Mercurias Americanus,* etc. New York: Prince Society Publication, 1876.

Women's Rights Collection (Mss.). The Schlesinger Library, The Radcliffe Institute, Cambridge, Mass.

Ziff, Larzer. *The Career of John Cotton.* Princeton: Princeton University Press, 1962.

Introduction

Few times in Europe's history have been as exciting or dangerous for the religious mind as the seventeenth century, the century of Blaise Pascal. In those days there were vast fields of knowledge still unmapped, and a man of genius could be an expert on science and mathematics, write treatises on theology, and—on a small investment of capital and energy—become a successful businessman, as well. The century that spanned from Galileo to Newton, however, was also a century of religious wars, inquisitions, and intense nationalism. Religious opinions and political loyalties were assumed to be closely connected, and too much interest in novel ideas rendered one's adherence to the perennial truths somewhat suspect.

Blaise Pascal lived in the midst of these countercurrents, and his life was swept by all of them. His father was a harried and unwelcome tax collector for the newly powerful French central government, but the family staked its fortune on the Richelieu government's bonds, and Blaise himself made an impact on the expanding commercial economy with his invention of a calculator. The mathematical theorist turned inventor and businessman also became a religious writer after his encounter with two pious physicians, and for a time the energy of Pascal's wide-ranging genius was concentrated on the religious community of Port Royal.

Pascal was perhaps the leading intellect at Port Royal, but the little community of followers of Bishop Jansen included many able and discerning spirits, including Pascal's sister. In the seventeenth century, of course, such a focusing of intellectual energy on one community, especially a community that followed novel methods in organization, pedagogy, and piety, aroused suspicion among religious authorities. Thus Pascal's deepest religious reflections were set in a context of controversy with church leaders who, in unsettled times, preferred a more conventional approach to religious truth.

In some ways, then, the most surprising fact about Pascal is that he was able to rise above the disorder and religious controversies of his time without attempting to evade them. Living in unsettled circumstances from the time of his mother's death during his infancy and beset by controversy that sometimes roused him to violent emotional responses, Pascal nonetheless sustained a high level of intellectual achievement and a calm, penetrating religious vision that always saw beyond the boundaries of the immediate controversy.

In this study, Brian Mahan guides us through the intricacies of Pascal's life with the aid of faith development theory. He shows the power of a highly developed faith to sustain itself against opposition and disorder and so makes Pascal's remote religious genius an intriguing sign of hope for our own time.

Brian Mahan is a graduate student of the Divinity School of the University of Chicago.

Toward Fire and Light:
The Faith of Blaise Pascal

Brian Mahan

Blaise Pascal was not only one of the great philosophers of his age but, with Newton and Toricelli, ranked as one of the most significant figures in the early development of the physical sciences. As a mathematician, he was without peer in France and rivaled by few in all of Europe. He was a master of French literary style, and T. S. Eliot thought that *The Provincial Letters* had established Pascal as the greatest of all satirists, "surpassed by none, not by Demosthenes, or Cicero, or Swift."

Pascal's philosophical and theological reflections are not, strictly speaking, systematic. The frequent observation that the character and quality of his life adds substance to his thought is certainly true. This interpenetration of action and reflection is evident, for instance, in the complex semantic structure of the *Pensees*. In this classic of Christian apologetic, Pascal refused to sacrifice either experiential intensity or cognitive integrity.

Pascal's worldly asceticism allowed him to accomplish a great deal, even while expecting and seeking little in return for his labors. Still Pascal was a man often in need of consolation, and others often came to him for consolation. His reactions at such times may be one of his greatest contributions. He never made for himself or for others prescriptions that involved facile promises of eternal bliss, never made maudlin prescriptions against hopelessness. For Pascal hope did not come cheaply; hope was able to grow, even to flourish, at the very edge of the abyss. Because of this quality of life—this quality of hopefulness dearly bought—Pascal was able to be a source of hope for others.

The Geometry of Hope

Pascal was born on June 19, 1623, in the town of Clermont, where his father's family had lived since the middle of the sixteenth century. Etienne, Blaise Pascal's father, had studied law in Paris. Sometime around 1616, he returned to Clermont and married Antoinette Begon, a woman eight years younger than he and also a product of the upper-middle class. The couple had three children. Blaise was the middle child and the only son. There was one sister, Gilberte, two years older than he; and another sister, Jacqueline, was two years younger. A year after Blaise Pascal's birth, the family moved into a large, century-old house in upper Clermont that was in bad repair.

Sickness and pain plagued Pascal during infancy and early childhood. At least twice his life was in danger: at birth he suffered convulsions, and in his second year he displayed a tendency toward listlessness that sometimes bordered on complete immobility. His mother was scarcely stronger than her son during those two years. She suffered from tuberculosis for some time before her death in 1626, when Pascal was three.

The ritual interaction between parent and child, "based on the periodicity of physical need, but also essential for emotional nourishment," was arbitrarily and frequently broken.[1] Hope, the "fundamental knowledge and feeling that there is a way out of difficulty,"[2] was not able to take root. The failure of hope during what should have been its foundational stage helps to explain

Pascal's frequent bouts with anxiety and ennui as he matured.

There has been a tendency among some biographers to isolate the experiences of Pascal's infancy and early childhood from his later life. Seeing his childhood in developmental perspective, it is possible to find a link between Pascal's concern for the plight of the individual lost in the chaos of existence, and his own desperate need for meaning and hope.

In 1534, when Pascal was eleven, the family moved to Paris. At the urging of Cardinal Richelieu, Pascal's father sold his law practice in Clermont and invested a large sum of money in government bonds. Living on the interest, he was able to divide the time formerly reserved for his profession between indulging his interest in mathematics and overseeing the education of his three children. Although a man of means, Étienne chose to care for his children himself. Louise Default, the housekeeper and governess, seems to have played only a minor role in their rearing.

Etienne Pascal believed that even the most fundamental operations and simplest explanations should be carefully presented to children according to the dictates of reason. He believed that the educational system devised and administered by the Jesuits, and ascendent at that time in France, was faulty since it placed a premium on memorization and habit and deprived the learner of the attainment of real understanding. The pedagogic principles of the father combined well with the exceptional learning abilities of the son. Blaise Pascal's penchant for "going to the very depths of things" had been noted by his sister and biographer, Gilberte, from as early as she could recall. At the age of eleven, Pascal wrote his first scientific treatise: Having noticed that he could mute the sound made by a spoon struck against a pewter plate merely by pressing it with his fingers, he chronicled his experimental findings in a short descriptive essay.

Although Blaise had mastered the elements of Greek and Latin grammar early and began to study Epictetus and Augustine under his father's direction, mathematics became his real passion. His father often would provoke his interest by challenging him to solve various geometric puzzles as the family sat at dinner. Never satisfied merely by finding the answer to a particular riddle, Pascal would press his father for explanations that would shed light on the relationships between mathematical operations and their resultants. Consistent with his educational ideal, Pascal's father at first sought to satisfy his son's appetite for mathematics. Soon, however, he felt obliged to evade his son's questions concerning geometric operations. He feared that Blaise might become confused by trying to comprehend complex ideas that he could not yet grasp, thus endangering whatever potential for mathematics he might possess. Pascal's father felt constrained to put his geometry books under lock and key. His fears were dispelled when, one afternoon in 1635, he entered a tiled room in his Paris home and found that his son had demonstrated to his own satisfaction that the sum of the angles in a triangle is equal to two right angles—theorem thirty-two in the forbidden materials.

Pascal's precocious achievements are especially significant because they represent early manifestations of his lifelong search for permanence in the midst of change. The floor of his father's study became more than a tiled floor. In its complex yet ordered patterns, Pascal could perceive a unity, a unity that seemed suddenly to appear from beneath the surface. A tendency toward belief was already emerging: where there was diversity, even chaos, proper discernment could find meaning and form.

Gilberte wrote that her brother would often pause in his calculations and whisper to himself, "How beautiful it is!"

Such momentary ecstasies, and the impassioned character of his probing and questioning mind, indicate that for Pascal the fruits of mathematical investigation were not wholly or even primarily cognitive. Intensive inquiry served to push against the horizon of his perception of the real, expanding his awareness of the possible. Mathematics was, before all else, an activity filled with hope, an activity that allowed Pascal to transcend the mundane without yielding to the impulse—first evident in that deathly languor of his second year of life—to escape the real by entirely giving it up. He discovered that reality was transcended not by turning away from it, but by scrutinizing it closely.

Calculators and Conic Sections

In 1638, when Blaise was fifteen, Etienne Pascal got himself into difficulty with Cardinal Richelieu by participating in a raucous demonstration with about four hundred other monied gentlemen who had invested heavily in government securities and now feared losing their investments as France's participation in the Thirty Years' War escalated. Many of the participants were arrested immediately and escorted to the Bastille, where they began serving indefinite sentences. Etienne Pascal escaped to Auvergne and emerged from hiding only after the Cardinal, under the spell of Jacqueline's poetry, declared her father a free man and granted him an audience on condition that he bring with him his daughter the poet and his son the mathematician.[3]

Richelieu, having learned of the elder Pascal's mathematical talents, assigned him to Rouen as inspector of taxes. The new position was a disaster. Mobs roamed the streets in open revolt against the government, and repeated confrontations between armed bands of locals and regular troops resulted in scores of deaths and injuries. Etienne Pascal was regarded by the people as a puppet for the central government. He was burdened with an almost impossible work load by his immediate superiors. He labored into the early morning hours each day in a fruitless attempt to keep his books in order.

Concerned for his father's health—and needing some project to help him avoid psychological surrender to the chaotic forces around him—Pascal set about the task of constructing a calculating machine. For two years he worked to construct and improve his brainchild. He assembled more than fifty workable models and finally succeeded in building the first mechanical calculator.

His fascination with the machine was as intense as his earlier fascination with pure mathematics. Determined that his labors not go unrewarded, he initiated an advertising campaign unlike any other of his time. Steinman describes an intriguing document written by Pascal, addressed to the prospective buyers:

> It is a commercial prospectus written in the purest publicity style and intended to attract customers. Pascal anticipates the customer's objections, starts a dialogue with him in the familiar style, holds up to admiration the marvelous qualities of his machine which is solid and durable and even able to stand up to the wear and tear of transport; "A simple, easy movement, convenient to open and quick to produce results."[4]

Pascal did not limit to the field of advertising his newly found ability to turn a phrase. According to Soltau, Pascal displayed a "love of discussion for its own sake" and "a desire to score points against an adversary, and a certain childish annoyance at being beaten or forestalled."[5]

He was not to be denied the opportunity to display his linguistic skills or his mathematical abilities. Pascal's father was one of a few permanent members of the Mersenne

Academy in Paris. At sixteen, Pascal presented his *Essay on Conic Sections,* a short treatise in which he formulated a new geometric theorem and proceeded to list for his audience four hundred propositions he had been able to deduce from it. Mersenne and Gassendi, two members of the small but exceptionally productive group, were moved to admiration; a third member, Rene Descartes, disconcerted by the performance of the novice, grumbled incoherently when asked for his opinion.

Port Royal

In 1646 Pascal's father slipped on a patch of ice and sustained a painful hip injury. Unable to reach the family physician, he was forced to trust two skilled but unlicensed medical practitioners. Both the twenty-three-year-old Pascal and his father quickly struck up a friendship with the two men, who it turned out, were ardent Christians and lay members of the religious community at Port Royal.

Port Royal des Champs, located about twenty miles from Paris, had been for centuries a convent for women of the Cistercian Order. In 1608, under the leadership of La Mere Angelique, a number of reforms had been initiated. The community became widely known because of the austere and pious life-style of its members. By 1625 the number of women in residence had increased from the twelve living there when La Mere Angelique had arrived, to over eighty. In 1638 La Mere Angelique brought M. de St. Cyran to Port Royal as director, and the community came under the influence of Jansenism. St. Cyran had attended the University of Louvain with Cornelius Jansen, who became Bishop of Ypres. The two shared deep admiration for the writings of St. Augustine and were intent upon reintroducing Augustine's thought into the mainstream of Roman Catholic theology. Jansen's book, *Augustinus,* was of central importance to this project, and during St. Cyran's tenure as director the book became especially significant to the members of the Port Royal community.

Blaise Pascal met with his friends from Port Royal while he set about the task of developing a more systematic understanding of the fundamentals of the Christian tradition. Pascal's studies centered on spiritual writers, both contemporary and medieval, and upon the Bible. It is not clear whether Pascal read *Augustinus* at this time, although it is amply clear that Jansenism, with its heavy stress upon the significance of original sin and the unreliability of human reason, colored his general outlook and influenced the course of his theological studies. Some members of the Port Royal community thought that scientific knowledge was a bitter fruit of human pride, and those members criticized Pascal for his continued interests in these subjects. Pascal heatedly defended his labors against such challenges.

It is obvious that the realm of the sacred took on new and more powerful significance for Pascal in wake of the events of 1646. This change is often referred to as his "first conversion." Such a designation is open to question. It is true that religion was now granted a more prominent position in his life, but it is important to note that this new interest did not replace his speculative activities. It seems more accurate to interpret Pascal's religious faith as taking its place alongside his mathematical and scientific interests as an additional source of meaning and hope.

The faith that suddenly became so prominent in Pascal's life at twenty-three had its own distinct history and developmental sequence; it did not appear suddenly. In seventeenth-century France, it was customary for infants to be baptized eight days after birth. Pascal had been baptized in accordance with custom, and his father had accepted the responsibility of nurturing his son's faith. Gilberte wrote that her father "had always a great respect for religion and had inculcated it to us, particularly to my brother, giving him the fundamental idea that everything which is of faith can in no sense fall under the control of reason."[6]

During the same period that young Pascal was beginning to barrage his father with questions about mathematical operations, he began also to question him about God and about the religious ceremonies they attended together each week. If his father's answers to his questions about geometry could be evasive, his answers to questions about religion were mystifying. Religion, his father thought, was simply not to be talked about. Although very little can be documented concerning the details of Pascal's childhood religious education, it can be assumed that he was initiated into sacramental worship and that he received formal instruction before receiving the sacraments of penance, confirmation, and the Eucharist.

Apparently Pascal never thought to question the authority of the Church in matters of faith and morals; it seems also that he never broke the pattern of worship that was established in his early youth. Given the mysteries of the Mass and his father's silent but deeply felt reverence for the sacred, it is not difficult to understand how Pascal later came to see religion as a deep source of meaning.

Still, it is clear that during his adolescence religion was no more than a secondary source of meaning. The "conversion" of 1646 really signified the reestablishment of religion as a mediator of meaning in his life. After this reestablishment, Pascal possessed a new perspective from which to examine the world. "Blaise realized that some men watched the movement of the soul with the same meticulous precision that he had applied to the regulation of the wheels of his calculating machine."[7]

Pascal would not allow his commitment to science to disappear in a fog of faith. Many of his most significant scientific contributions were made at the very time he was being pressured by some of his more zealous comrades at Port Royal to disavow what they saw as pretension and worldly ambition. It was during this time that Pascal, by refining certain experiments first undertaken by Toricelli, was able to establish the correlation between changes in altitude and variations in air pressure.

Between Two Worlds

Pascal's father died in 1651. Blaise was twenty-eight. Within a year of his father's death, he and his younger sister, Jacqueline, had a falling out. The conflict arose because Pascal felt that his sister's decision to take final vows at Port Royal dishonored their father's often expressed wish that Jacqueline not enter the convent. The inordinate vehemence of his reaction to her plans cannot be explained solely in terms of his role as loyal son and responsible brother. For Pascal, his sister's decision must have signified the final dissolution of an exceptionally supportive family structure. In addition, Pascal stood to lose a large portion of the family inheritance if Jacqueline took the veil. This financial loss was significant because it threatened to bring to an end a life-style that had allowed him ample time for research and reflection. Most significant, Jacqueline's unconditional commitment to the community at Port Royal challenged Pascal's understanding of his own faith. Twenty-nine and clinging desperately—and less certainly—to his belief that Christian faith and worldly vocation were not mutually exclusive, he must have viewed his faith as a fragile and ephemeral thing by comparison to his sister's all-consuming, other worldly passion.

This troubling issue was not resolved at once. Between 1652 and 1654 Pascal continued his search for a "worldly philosophy" that might help him integrate action and belief. Under the tutelage of his close friend the Duc de

Roannes and another companion, Chevalier de Mere, Pascal immersed himself in the life-style and writings of the Freethinkers. Of those whose writings he read most attentively, Montaigne had the deepest influence. T. S. Eliot suggests that "by the time a man knew Montaigne well enough to attack him, he would already be thoroughly infected."[8] Eliot's estimation of the importance of Montaigne for Pascal is correct, but his assertion that Pascal read Montaigne with the intention of demolishing him seems as misplaced as Soltau's converse assertion that Pascal's period of searching represents the embodiment of a "spiritual coldness" that had taken hold as a result of his "care for the world" and "the deceitfulness of riches."[9] It is true, however, that Pascal tried to maintain his relationship with the community at Port Royal while trying to learn what he could from his contact with the luminaries of secular society.

A Fire is Kindled

By late in the summer of 1654, it was obvious to Pascal that his search for unity of vocation and faith could not find its focus in a worldly philosophy. At thirty-one his search for a solid and permanent base for his work and faith shifted back to the community at Port Royal, and especially to the person of his sister Jacqueline. In September, he began to visit her more frequently than during the past few years. Later in the fall, confessing his need for spiritual guidance and practical advice, Pascal became a daily visitor at Port Royal. During this time, Jacqueline displayed a profound understanding of her "proud and wounded" brother:

He was conscious of an urge to abandon everything; that owing to an extreme aversion for the follies and distractions of society and a continual sense of guilt, he felt detached from all those things in a manner quite unlike anything he had experienced before; but that he felt himself so abandoned, that he was not conscious of any inclination to turn to God; that he had tried with all his strength, but was aware that it was much more his own reason and his own mind which forced him in what he knew to be the right direction, and not the action of God.[10]

Feeling abandoned by God and unable to derive satisfaction from his work, Pascal judged himself harshly. He confided to Jacqueline that he "must certainly have been terribly attached to worldly things" and that selfishness had enabled him "to resist the graces that God sent him and to turn a deaf ear to His appeal."

On November 23, 1654, the dark night of doubt gave way to dazzling light. He had been reading John's account of the Passion, reflecting on Jesus' acceptance of his former disciples as his friends and on his prayer that each one "be sanctified in truth." Truth came to Pascal as fire:

God of Abraham, God of Isaac, God of Jacob, Not of philosophers and scholars, Certainty, Joy, Certainty, Feeling, Light, Joy. God of Jesus-Christ, Deum meum et Deum vestrum (John xx 17)
Thy God will be my God (Ruth)
Forgetting of the world and of all save God.
He is only to be found in the ways taught in the Gospel.
Greatness of the human soul.
O righteous Father, the world has not known Thee, but I have known Thee (John xvii)
Joy, joy and tears of joy.
I have become separated from him,
Derelinquerunt me fontes aquae vivae.
"My God wilt thou forsake me?"
"This is eternal life, that they may know thee the only true God and him thou hast sent, Jesus Christ."
Jesus-Christ.
Jesus-Christ.

I have become separated from him. I have fled from him,
renounced him, crucified him.
May I never be separated from him.
He is only to be kept by the ways taught in the Gospel.
Total and sweet renunciation-surrender.
Total submission to Jesus-Christ and to my director.
Eternally in joy for one day's trial on earth.
Non obliviscar sermones tuos. Amen.

It is not until January 7, a month and a half after that
night of fire, that any substantial change in Pascal's
life-style can be perceived. On that day, Pascal, then
thirty-two, entered the community at Port Royal for an
extended retreat. There he kept to a strict schedule, rising
at three for matins, attending Mass at six, working and
contemplating during the daylight hours, and retiring for
the night at seven. Pascal at this point abandoned himself
entirely to the faith and submitted obediently to the
instruction of his spiritual advisor, Abbe Singlin.

The Provincial Letters

As the new spiritual roots took hold, Pascal experienced
a growing sense of inner peace. His peace was short-lived.
On January 31, 1655, the Abbe Rocote refused to grant
absolution to the Duc de Leancourt, apparently because he
had sent his daughter to boarding school at Port Royal.
Reprisals of this kind against supporters of the community
had become increasingly common since the Papal Bull of
1653, in which five propositions in Jansen's *Augustinus*
were condemned. Four of the five condemned propositions dealt explicitly with the relationship between grace
and liberty. Rome felt Jansen had come dangerously close
to denying the cooperative role played by free will in
actualizing the power of supernatural grace. Nor was
criticism of the community at Port Royal limited to the

Church hierarchy: Many persons in France—scholars and common folk alike—thought that Jansenism represented either an "obedience-lacking Catholicism" or a "courage-lacking Protestantism."

Supporters of the community quickly saw the need for recasting Port Royal's image. With the approval of the community, Antoine Arnauld defended *Augustinus* by arguing that the five propositions condemned in the Bull should indeed be condemned but that they could not be found in Jansen's book. Arnauld's dry, academic writing had little impact on public opinion.

In July of 1655, Pascal suggested that he might help to formulate a strategy for a published defense. The community greeted his offer with enthusiasm, and on January 23, 1656, the first of the eighteen *Provincial Letters* was published. In this first letter, Pascal defended Arnauld against scholars at the Sorbonne who wished to have his interpretation of *Augustinus* condemned. Pascal's persuasive writing quickly transformed public opinion. His dual strategy was to play down the significance of the problem while poking fun at the theology faculty of the Sorbonne:

We were entirely mistaken. It was only yesterday that I was undeceived. Until that time I had laboured under the impression that the disputes in the Sorbonne were vastly important, and deeply affected the interests of religion. The frequent convocations of an assembly so illustrious as that of the Theological faculty of Paris, attended by so many extraordinary and unprecedented circumstances, led one to form such high expectations that it was impossible to help coming to the conclusion that the subject was most extraordinary. You will be greatly surprised however when you learn . . .[11]

Pascal was also adept at uncovering and mimicking weaknesses in his adversaries. He was especially fond of spoofing pedantry:

"Hold there," said he, "One must be a theologian to see the point of this question. The difference between us is so subtle that it is with some difficulty we can discern it ourselves—you will find it rather too much for your powers of comprehension. Content yourself with knowing that it is very true that the Jansenists will tell you that all the righteous have always the power of obeying the commandments; that is not the point of the dispute between us; but mark you, they will not tell you that the power is proximate. That is the point."[12]

In the fifth letter, Pascal attacked the Jesuits for promulgating probabilism. According to the theory of probabilism, in matters where there is no certainty about the moral status of an act, the citing of one established authority affords sufficient grounds for judging, and even for acting, in a manner inconsistent with other interpretations of moral law. Action based on such authority could proceed even when the variant interpretation had no additional authoritative support.

"So it would appear," I observed with a smile, "that a single doctor may turn consciences round about and upside down as he pleases, and yet land them in safe position."

"You must not laugh at it, sir," returned the Monk . . .
"Now the authority of a learned and pious man is entitled to a very great consideration; because (mark the reason), if the testimony of such a man has great influence in convincing us that such and such an event occurred, say at Rome, for example, why should it not have the same weight in a question of morals?"

"An odd comparison this," interrupted I . . .[13]

Pascal wrote the series of letters under the pen name "Montalte." Letter 17 is a response to Father Annat's accusation that Montalte himself is a heretic; in this letter one can perceive a sense of frustration and anger not present in earlier letters. Additionally, it gives us some idea of Pascal's impression of his relationship with Port Royal and with the Catholic Church early in 1657:

> Certain it is, Father, that I have not said a word in behalf of those impious propositions, which I detest with all my heart. And even though Port Royal should hold them, I protest against your drawing any conclusion from this against me, as, thank God, I have no sort of connection with any community except the Catholic, Apostolic and Roman Church, in the bosom of which I desire to live and die, and beyond the pale of which I am persuaded there is no salvation.[14]

Later in 1657, Pope Alexander VII condemned the five Jansenist propositions, condemning them precisely as they appeared in *Augustinus*. In the eighteenth letter, Pascal tried to continue the debate while avoiding the language condemned in the Bull, resorting to the same kind of convoluted reasoning he had earlier parodied.

Stages in Faith

When Pascal's faith is understood in developmental terms, it is possible to see the "conversions" of 1646 and 1654 in a wider context. Both experiences marked turning points in Pascal's life, but each was also part of his lifelong struggle for hope against despair and order against chaos. In that longer trajectory, it was the experiences of fire and light in 1654 that showed Pascal the way to a new faith orientation.

Blaise Pascal, the precocious geometer and mathematician, seems also to have entered early into the activities of observing, ordering, and unifying that are essential to a synthetic-conventional faith. Pascal's essay on the nature of sound, written when he was eleven, typifies his early development of the operations associated with this faith stage. By the time he first addressed the Mersenne Academy, at age sixteen, the cognitive prerequisites of synthetic-conventional faith were surely well developed. The structuring activity that is faith, however, involves more than cognitive sophistication. It involves a resting of the heart, a commitment of the total person, a centering of the affections. The young Pascal, emotionally wounded by the sicknesses he and his mother experienced in his infancy, and by her early death, took a long time to consolidate the comprehensive synthesis that grounds identity and faith in stage 3.

Hazelton's description of Pascal as "conventionally religious, untouched by either skepticism or enthusiasm"—a comment intended to describe Pascal's faith prior to his "first conversion"—seems equally descriptive of Pascal's faith after the restoration of religion as a matter of importance in his life. There is the temptation to interpret Pascal's early enthusiasm for the Port Royal community as the onset of the individuative-reflective stage; in this perspective, the two young men from the community who treated his father might be seen as charismatic representatives of an attractive ideological option that provided Pascal, at twenty-two, with enough raw material for the effective internalization of a personal world synthesis. There is sufficient evidence, however, to suggest that such individuating faith did not take form until after the 1654 conversion, when he experienced faith as entirely new and uniquely his own.

Until his death in 1651, Pascal's father was the dominant influence in his life. It was probably not until his father's death that Pascal's synthetic-conventional faith was shaken deeply, although his interactions with members of the Port Royal community probably had rattled it. Three weeks after his father's death, Pascal wrote a letter to Gilberte that confirms the overpowering influence of his father:

> It seems to me that he is still alive . . . If I had lost him six years ago I would have been undone, and though I believe my need for him is less absolute today, I know that he would have been necessary to me ten years more and beneficial all my life.[15]

The second real jolt to Pascal's conventional faith occurred as a consequence of his struggle with Jacqueline. During this period, his inability to derive satisfaction from his mathematical and scientific work or from his desperate search for an adoptable world view among the freethinkers, or later at Port Royal, seems to indicate that the collapse of the synthetic-conventional stage was imminent. His hesitation to ratify his own investment in the community at Port Royal, which was exemplified in his keeping secret from his freethinking friends his visits to the Abbey, suggests that the individuative-reflective stage was not present fully until after Pascal settled into the regular disciplines of community life.

Pascal's vigorous search for meaning in the world and in his life prepared him for the conversion experience of 1654. Judging from his own description of this experience, it seems inadequate to describe his reaction as merely the ecstasy of discovery. The event seems more direct: Pascal seems to have felt as though, after his long search for meaning, meaning suddenly had sought him out and addressed him. His language is more the language of encounter than the language of discovery. Pascal's powerfully evocative memorial to the central revelational moment of his life is the work of a man in transition from synthetic-conventional faith to individuative-reflective faith. His powerful words, which demonstrate so clearly his stage of faith development, hint, through the imagery of love and total surrender, at another principle of dynamic change. A new vision began to direct his energies away from himself and toward the Other, of faith. It is not enough to describe Pascal's new faith as a higher integration of the old. His faith was not merely extended but transformed: he experienced new being.

Penseés

By the time the Jansenist controversy had run its course, Pascal's health had begun a final decline. In 1659 he wrote to his friend Fermat that he was required to walk with a cane and that he had not been able to keep up his work in geometry—now described as "only a profession." His failing health could not keep him from that profession very long. During 1659 he wrote several short treatises on pure mathematics and kept up his correspondence with several colleagues.

Despite his continued work in mathematics, the work that demanded the greatest investment of energy during this period was his Christian apologetic. *Pensees* is not a completed work; it probably is not even an outline of a single book. Since all the writings dealing with religion found in Pascal's study were bound after his death into one volume, it is probable that *Pensees* contains material Pascal did not intend to be a part of his finished apology.

From as early as 1658, when he addressed a group of Port Royalists for two hours about his forthcoming "Vindication of Christianity," Pascal indicated that his work was intended primarily for the worldly skeptic. This approach was unusual for Pascal's time. Believers and skeptics inhabited mutually hostile camps; a favorite tactic of the militant believer was to ignore or even to deny the existence of freethinkers. Estimates of the number of freethinkers in France illustrate the common approach— they fluctuate according to the degree of import the estimator wished to assign to their presence. Father Mersenne estimated that fifty thousand lived in Paris alone, while Father Garassee estimated not more than five declared atheists in all of France—three Italians and two Frenchmen.

Central to Pascal's appeal to the skeptic is his portrayal of the place of the individual in the world:

> Let man then contemplate the whole of nature in her full and grand majesty and turn his vision from the low objects which surround him. Let him gaze on that brilliant light, set like an eternal lamp to illumine the universe; let the earth appear to him a point in comparison with that described by the stars in their revolution round the firmament.
>
> But if our view be arrested there, let our imagination pass beyond; it will sooner exhaust the power of conception than nature that of supplying material of conception. The whole visible world is only an imperceptible atom in the ample bosom of nature. . . . In short, it is the greatest sensible mark of the almighty Power of God, that imagination loses itself in that thought.
>
> Returning to himself, let man consider what he is in comparison with all existence; let him regard himself as lost in this remote corner of nature. . . . What is a man in the Infinite?
>
> But show him another prodigy equally astonishing, let him examine the most delicate thing he knows. Let a mite be given him, with its minute body and parts incomparably more minute, limbs with their joints, veins in the limbs, blood in the veins, humours in the blood, drops in the humours, vapours in the drops. . . . Let him lose himself in wonders as amazing in their vastness. . . . He who regards himself in this light will be afraid of himself, and observing himself sustained in the body given him by nature between those two abysses of the Infinite and Nothing will tremble at the sight of these marvels.[16]

Pascal saw the individual "limited in every way." One lived in a state of impotence, not able to "achieve the absolute, but, at the same time, . . . [not able] . . . to remain satisfied with any understanding that does not strive after it." One was left in a state of perpetual tension; "we burn with the desire to find solid ground and an ultimate sure foundation whereon to build . . .," yet consistently "our whole groundwork cracks, and the earth opens to abysses."[17] Still, happiness is possible; just as cosmic opposites unite, so do the polar tensions of the individual find themselves conjoined in an uncertain affirmation of certainty:

> The Stoics say, "retire within yourselves; it is there you will find your rest." And that is not true.
>
> Others say, "Go out of yourselves; seek happiness in amusement," and that is not true. Illness comes.
>
> Happiness is neither without us nor within us. It is within God, both within us and without us.[18]

Pascal's estimation of humanity's place in the world is perhaps most vividly drawn in fragment 434:

> What a chimera then is man! What a novelty! What a monster, what a chaos, what a contradiction. What a prodigy! Judge of all things, imbecile worm of the earth, depository of truth, a sink of uncertainty and error; the pride and refuse of the universe.

Marxist literary critic Lucien Goldmann has demonstrated how Pascal's paradoxical affirmation of the human condition moves beyond the "cosmic dualism" espoused by members of the community at Port Royal. The world-synthesis he had acquired from the community enabled Pascal to move more comfortably in the outside world than his fellow Port Royalists who held the world to be evil in all its aspects. Goldmann's language almost echoes the language of faith development theory when making distinctions between the structures of individuative-reflective and paradoxical-consolidative faith:

> The position of Barcos [member of Port Royal community] is, in effect, a dualistic one: on the one hand, there is the evil, paradoxical and contradictory world from which God is absent; and on the other hand, there is the clear, certain and unambiguous universe of the divinity. The ethic which he deduces from this is simple and straight-forward; evil consists of wanting to live in the world, and goodness of withdrawing into solitude, into the divine universe and, in the final analysis, into death.
>
> Pascal, on the other hand, goes a long way towards transcending this dualism when he extends the paradox from the world of man to God. For Barcos, God exists in absolute certainty; for Pascal, God exists in an uncertain certainty, in a wager. . . . Barcos' dualism enables him to withdraw from the world and seek refuge in solitude. Pascal evolved naturally from the idea of the wager to the paradoxical position whereby he lived in the world but at the same time refused it.[19]

While any number of passages gleaned from *Pensees* would seem to corroborate Goldmann's judgment that Pascal moved beyond the "cosmic duality" characterized by the Port Royalists, it is not proper to draw a simple equation between the content of *Pensees* and the understanding Pascal had of his own faith. One must also attend to the concrete events of the final years of his life.

By late 1659, pain had become Pascal's constant companion; his life was increasingly marked by severe austerity; whatever he did not need, he discarded. Whatever redeemable time he had available, he spent in prayer or in performing acts of charity. Pascal formed a working relationship with Maignant de Berniers, who had recently become an assistant to St. Vincent de Paul. He raised funds for de Berniers and accompanied him to the hospitals and the hovels where those most in need of attention and solace were to be found.

Soon Pascal was dragged back into the harsh world of Church politics. In the fall of 1660, the French Church hierarchy, led by Cardinal Marozin, decided to destroy the Jansenist threat once and for all; Louis XIV lent support. The earlier condemnation of the five Jansenist propositions was reissued and circulated among ecclesiastics and teachers of theology. Port Royal was divided on how best to counter this new assault. De Saci, Barcos, and others felt that no defense was necessary and pleaded for church unity. Pascal sided with Arnauld and Nicole, favoring confrontation. Most of the members thought it wise to sign quietly the document rejecting Jansenism; of those living at the Abbey, only Jacqueline and one other Sister refused to sign.[20] At a meeting in his home, Pascal fainted when he realized that he was virtually alone in his desire to defend Jansen's *Augustinus* and the worldview that was associated with it. Shortly afterward, he too bowed to Church authority. He later confided to Father Beaurrier, his last confessor, that he did not know whether he had spoken too much or too little in his jousts with the hierarchy.

Pascal returned to his quiet ministry of prayer and service. C. S. MacKenzie writes that Pascal acquired a copy of Fr. Matial du Mans' *Spiritual Almanac* containing an extensive listing of the religious services taking place in Paris, and that he walked from church to church, across the length and breadth of the city as though on a holy pilgrimage.[21]

His work with the downtrodden continued. He accepted one indigent family, the Bardouts, into his own home; in the summer of 1662, when one of the children came down with smallpox, he stayed with Gilberte so that the child would not have to be sent to a hospital for the poor.

As the summer progressed, Pascal's health degenerated more rapidly. By early August he was gravely ill and was visited by many of the best physicians in Paris, all predicting a quick recovery. The optimism of the physicans was more a product of professional competitiveness than of informed judgment. On August 17, Pascal complained of an "extraordinary headache" and asked that a priest be summoned so that he might receive Holy Communion before dying. The doctors apparently cajoled the family into ignoring Pascal's plea. In response, Pascal stated that since he was to be denied communion with the Head of the Church he wanted to enjoy communion with one of its members, asking that someone poor and needing medical attention to be placed in the room with him and given the same quality of treatment he was receiving. This request, too, was denied. A priest was finally summoned in time to administer the last rights of the Church. Soon afterward, Pascal died.

A brief reflection written by Pascal three years before his death speaks deeply of his commitment, a commitment that never waned, a commitment fulfilled in his death:

> I do not ask for health or sickness or life or death: I ask that you dispose of my health and sickness, my life and my death, for your glory, for my salvation, and for the use of the Church and your saints of which I am part. You alone know what you wish. Give to me, take away from me; but make my will conform to yours: that in humble and perfect state of submission and in holy trust, I may prepare myself to receive the commands of your eternal Providence; and that I adore equally all that comes to me from you.[22]

Bibliography

Caillet, Emile. *Pascal, Genius in the Light of Scripture.* Philadelphia: Westminster Press, 1945.

Chevalier, Jacques. *Pascal.* Trans. Lilian A. Clark. London: Longmans, Green and Co., 1930.

Clark, William. *Pascal and the Port Royalists.* Edinburgh: T. & T. Clark.

Collins, James. *God in Modern Philosophy.* New York: Henry Regney Co., 1959.

Eastwood, D. M. *The Revival of Pascal.* New York: Oxford University Press, 1936.

Erikson, Erik. *The Ontogeny of Ritualization,* in Donald R. Cutler, ed., *The Religious Situation,* 1968. Boston: Beacon Press, 1968.

Goldmann, Lucien. *The Hidden God.* Trans. Philip Thody. London: Routledge & Kegan Paul, 1970.

Hazelton, Roger. *Blaise Pascal, The Genius of his Thought.* Philadelphia: Westminister Press, 1974.

Lynch, William F. *Images of Hope.* London: University of Notre Dame Press, 1974.

MacKenzie, Charles. *Pascal's Anguish and Joy.* New York: Philosophical Library, 1973.

Pascal, Blaise. *Pensees.* Intro. by T. S. Eliot. New York: E. P. Dutton, 1958.

———*The Provincial Letters,* in *Pascal.* Trans. W. F. Trotter, vol. 33, *Great Books of the Western World.* Chicago: Encyclopaedia Britannica, 1952.

———*The Miscellaneous Writings.* Trans. M. P. Faugere, Intro. by George Brown. London: Longmans, Green and Co., 1944.

Soltau, Roger. *Pascal: The Man and His Message.* West Point, Conn.:, Greenwood Press, 1970.

Introduction

Not every faith perspective is expressed in specifically religious terms, but through the lenses of a faith development theory many works of human genius express a religious dimension in the lives of their creators. Rarely is this so clear as in the case of Ludwig Wittgenstein, an Austrian philosopher whose exploration of the structures of language that form the horizon of our experience also provided the structure and set the limits for his own life.

Wittgenstein's works are central documents of twentieth-century philosophy, but few persons who read them understand how much these writings were part of a man's struggle to conform his life and will to the shape of the reality he saw. Behind the terse, lucid, and logical structure of his writings, one encounters a man who admired the mystical Christianity of Tolstoy, the rigorous ethical demands of the Sermon on the Mount, and the penetrating wit of Kierkegaard, who—like Wittgenstein himself—took up the pen to show his comfortable compatriots the uncomfortable truth about themselves. The philosophical writings that Wittgenstein's British colleagues mistook for purely theoretical studies in logic were for the author a passionate attempt to speak his commitments meaningfully.

It is the reflexive impact of the theoretical study on the theoretician's life that marks Wittgenstein's philosophical progress as a trajectory in faith. In the long space between his two great works, the *Tractatus* (first published in 1921) and the

Philosophical Investigations (completed in 1936), we see Wittgenstein first struggling unsuccessfully to conform his life to a narrow and rigid philosophical framework and then searching for a style that would allow him to live out his demanding personal commitment in a world that offered many more possibilities than he first realized.

Linell Cady, a doctoral candidate in theology at Harvard, avoids the temptation to portray Wittgenstein as a crypto-Christian. His ardent rejection of any forgiveness for the moral failures he so keenly felt forecloses that interpretation. Rather, this biographical sketch concentrates on displaying Wittgenstein's investment of himself in his philosophy. A man of great wealth who lived very simply, a lonely man who inspired intense personal loyalty, Wittgenstein lived a life of commitment, discipline, and sacrifice that reminds one more of an eremitic saint than of a university scholar. That this man could close his arduous and often unhappy search with the words, "Tell them I've had a wonderful life," bespeaks a discovery of more than academic significance. There is something to be learned here about kingdoms that are not of this world.

The Philosophical Passion of Ludwig Wittgenstein

Linell Cady

A Family and Its City

Ludwig Wittgenstein was born in 1889, the last of Karl and Leopoldine Wittgenstein's nine children. A family prominent in Viennese society, the Wittgensteins were very much at the center of the cultural life of the city during the closing decades of the Habsburg Empire, entertaining such notables in the arts as Clara Schumann, Pablo Casals, and Johannes Brahms.[1]

The children of the family were exposed to the arts through their mother's commitment to cultural life, and they were exposed to the pragmatic interests of business by their father—a self-made millionaire who amassed a fortune creating the iron and steel industries in what is now Czechoslovakia. These dual familial concerns for the arts and for business deeply influenced Ludwig Wittgenstein in his adult choices of which philosophical problems to address.

Each member of the Wittgenstein family was highly gifted. Despite the loss of his right arm in the First World War, Ludwig's older brother Paul pursued a successful career as a pianist. Their sister Margarete was widely involved in Viennese artistic and cultural life and had a sophisticated understanding of German philosophy. Even as children, these siblings were gifted. Ludwig also

121

displayed genuine creativity: when he was ten years old, he constructed a working sewing machine of matchsticks. Nevertheless, because of the remarkable cultural and artistic manifestations of talent in the rest of the family, his genius was never regarded as peculiarly outstanding.

Karl Wittgenstein ruled the family in autocratic fashion, expecting his chilren to defer to his judgments concerning their education and careers. The resulting tension between father and sons led to a series of tragic events. Hans, the eldest son, wanted to pursue a career in medicine, and had outstanding aptitude for medical study; because Karl wanted his son to be a businessman, he refused permission for studies in medicine. As Karl Wittgenstein himself had done a generation earlier when *his* father had opposed his own career choice, Hans went to America to escape paternal influence. In 1902, still in America, Hans Wittgenstein committed suicide. Karl Wittgenstein's stubborn manner was not altered by this tragedy; in 1904, under similar conditions, a second son, Rudi, committed suicide.

Like his two older brothers who had committed suicide, Ludwig Wittgenstein was homosexual. Conflicts over his sexual identity were a continual source of guilt and self-loathing throughout his life. Intermittently, he would engage in furtive, promiscuous encounters with men he met in bars in Vienna and London, then try to alleviate his despair by secluding himself—sometimes in remote areas of Norway or in small Austrian villages.[2]

In the Wittgenstein household, there was no religious unity. Ludwig Wittgenstein's paternal grandfather had converted from Judaism to Protestantism. Ludwig's mother, Leopoldine, was Roman Catholic, and Ludwig was baptized Catholic; until the First World War, he listed Catholicism as his religion. From his father's strict sense of moral duty and obsessive devotion to his work, Ludwig

Wittgenstein acquired a similar sense of duty and devotion to work. Although there is no direct mention of religious education, a remark made by Wittgenstein in a lecture suggests certain results of his early exposure to religion:

> If the question arises as to the existence of a god or God, it plays an entirely different role to that of the existence of any person or object I ever heard of. One said, had to say, that one *believed* in the existence, and if one did not believe, this was regarded as something bad. Normally if I did not believe in the existence of something no one would think there was anything wrong in this.[3]

Although information about Wittgenstein's early years is not very detailed, certain of his character traits suggest that he may not have experienced during his early years the kinds of nurturing relationships or the kinds of environments that might have enabled him to form a fundamental trusting attitude toward life. Throughout his life he displayed ambivalence toward beliefs, friends, and work. Often suspicious of his friends, he would claim that they liked him only for the ways his philosophy could be useful to them. Yet he valued his close friendships and devoted much energy to continuing them. Sometimes he considered his work valuable and was afraid that it might be destroyed by fire before it could be published; at other times, he expressed belief that his work was not valuable and that it could be of no practical use to anyone. He was capable of displaying a brash arrogance—and of expressing an apparently sincere belief in his failure as a human being. High self-esteem mingled with disgust, while contradictory, were combined to give him an explosive personality that was an energizer of creativity as well as destructive of inner peace.

Consideration of Wittgenstein's early environment may help to explain these ambivalences. He was the last-born child of the family, seven of his eight siblings living beyond infancy. It seems reasonable to suggest that by the time he was born, his mother was not enthusiastic about caring for yet another child, but far more interested in pursuing her musical and artistic interests. Although there were plenty of nurses, governesses, and hired servants in the household, Ludwig may have received less personal care and affection than he needed in order to develop a trusting orientation toward life.

While his mother pursued her cultural interests, his father engaged in commercial ventures. Although Karl Wittgenstein did not spend much time with his children, he played a decisive role in the shaping of Ludwig's attitudes. It is interesting that in his later life, Ludwig Wittgenstein showed little interest in religious beliefs and practices but retained a strong sense of moral duty—a basic attitude he got from his father.

As a child develops, his environment enlarges to include peer-group influences as well as parental influences. For Ludwig, this did not occur early. His father thought that the only way to obtain a first-rate education was through private tutors. Until he was fourteen, Ludwig was educated at home and deprived of the wider social environment typical for a school-age child. This heightened his dependency on his family and contributed to a lifelong uneasiness among nonfamily groups.

The suicides in 1902 and 1904 of Ludwig's two older brothers occurred when he was thirteen and fifteen, a period in his life when he was attempting to coordinate the various spheres of home, school, and peers into some order. Wittgenstein had to deal not just with the tragic deaths of two brothers, but also with the fact that the deaths were self-inflicted and that they appeared to be responses to disagreements with his autocratic and demanding father. Wittgenstein later related to a friend that this time marked the beginning of a very difficult period for him during which he was not often happy. When it is remembered that Wittgenstein was quite often unhappy during his life, it is particularly telling that he remembered this as an exceptionally unhappy time.

We can only speculate on the impact the suicides may have had on the young Wittgenstein. He may have felt keenly the inadequacy of religion for explaining such events and therefore would have resorted to an affective response that he could not easily articulate. Throughout his life he saw religion as something that became manifest in activities rather than as beliefs that could be expressed verbally. This view of religion may have had its roots in his struggling with the emotional conflict rising out of his brother's suicides. Beyond this speculation, we know that Leopoldine Wittgenstein went into a prolonged period of depression because of the suicides of her two sons. This reaction by his mother increased Ludwig's bitter sense of aloneness even while he tried to cope with these traumatic events in his own mind.

In 1908, when he was nineteen, Wittgenstein finished his secondary schooling and decided to attend the University of Manchester to study engineering. By this time he had wide exposure to the intellectual and artistic interests of Viennese society, even though he spent most of his time in the confines of the Wittgenstein household.

Margarete had introduced him to the writings of Schopenhauer, whose interpretation of Kant was very popular in Viennese circles. Schopenhauer criticized the Kantian duality of theoretical and practical reason, by which Kant had attempted to provide a rational foundation for ethics. Schopenhauer argued that morality was distinct from reason, located more in feeling and in intention than in intellect.

Another thinker popular in Viennese society was Søren

Kierkegaard, who extended Schopenhauer's separation of reason and morality into an antithesis so radical that it must be regarded as paradox. Wittgenstein always remained attracted to Kierkegaard and the anti-rationalistic position that he represented.

> The process which Kant had set in motion by distinguishing the "speculative" and the "practical" functions of reason, and which Schopenhauer kept moving by separating the world as representation from the world as will, culminated in Kierkegaard's total separation of reason from anything that pertains to the meaning of life.[4]

There was also popular in Vienna another philosophical school quite different from that of Schopenhauer and Kierkegaard, a positivist philosophy based on the data of sense perceptions, which tended to focus on the natural sciences and to exclude other philosophical concerns, such as ethics. Fritz Mauthner had attempted to combine these two philosophical strains through a critique of language. His attempts resulted in a radical skepticism in which not only the ethical but also the scientific enterprise was muffled into a mystical silence. Wittgenstein could not accept this skepticism in regard to the physical sciences; he was convinced of the ability of certain sciences—particularly mechanics—to represent reality accurately through mathematical formulations. Wittgenstein's plans to study engineering reflected his acceptance of the scientific enterprise as a valid one. To study engineering in Vienna at this time involved not only technical study but required also the mastery of physics and analysis of the ways in which theories related to reality.

When Wittgenstein left Vienna to study engineering in England, he had already been strongly influenced by widely differing philosophical traditions. It seems that he kept these influences in a sort of equilibrium as he left home. He soon would show signs that the various attitudes he had apprehended from Viennese cultural life were being reformed into a new position that would be expressed in the *Tractatus.*

The Logic of Friendship and Loneliness

During his first year at the University of Manchester, he concentrated upon aeronautics; however, soon after, his interest quickly turned to the mathematics of engineering and then to the foundations of mathematics. Wanting to know whether there was such a subject as "the foundations of mathematics," he was advised to study Russell and Whitehead's *Principia mathematica.* This work influenced him deeply and led him to the works of Frege, a well-known logician. In 1912 he went to Cambridge to study with Russell. Toward the end of 1913, when he was twenty-four, he went to Norway to work in solitude on the problems of logic that intrigued him. He continued this work until the outbreak of the war in August, 1914.

His activities suggest that the study of logic was at the center of his life during these six years. That, in fact, is how most of his biographers have interpreted these years. There are indications in his letters and notebooks, however, that from the beginning his logical investigations had cultural and ethical foundations. Janik and Toulmin have argued convincingly that Wittgenstein came to the logic of Frege and Russell with philosophical concerns that were products of Viennese culture. He found in logic a tool for addressing questions he had formed prior to coming to England: He was trying to express through logical theory a world where scientific investigation and the work of ethics could coexist.

It is clear from his correspondence that he was vitally interested in ethical and religious issues even while he was studying formal logic. In several letters to Russell, he approvingly refers to James' *Varieties of Religious Experience:*

> Whenever I have time now I read James' *Varieties of Religious Experience.* This book does me a lot of good. I don't mean to say that I will be a saint soon, but I am not sure that it does not improve me a little in a way which I would like to improve very much.[5]

The years in England (1908–1914) mark Wittgenstein's transition between stage 3 and stage 4 as articulated in faith development theory. He was finding it increasingly difficult to keep various aspects of reality tightly compartmentalized. It was not an easy transition for Wittgenstein:

> My day passes between logic, whistling, going for walks, and being depressed. I wish to God that I were more intelligent and everything would finally become clear to me—or else that I needn't live much longer.[6]

The transition Wittgenstein was making is illustrated in his relationship with Bertrand Russell. When they first met in 1912, they formed a close friendship based mainly on their mutual interest in formal logic. Russell recognized Wittgenstein's genius and soon was treating him as an equal in philosophical discourse. Russell felt that "getting to know Wittgenstein was one of the most exciting intellectual adventures of my life."[7]

For a while, Wittgenstein was willing to participate in a friendship based primarily on mutual intellectual concern; soon however, this basis for friendship was shown to be inadequate. Wittgenstein exposed his inner torments to Russell during several meetings, but Russell was not much help with these personal struggles. Russell relates that Wittgenstein came to his rooms one evening and announced that as soon as he left Russell, he intended to commit suicide. Because of this announcement, Russell did not want him to go. After an hour or two of total silence, Russell asked, "Wittgenstein, are you thinking about logic or about your sins?" "Both," he said, and then reverted to silence.[8]

Wittgenstein came gradually to feel that his friendship with Russell, limited as it was to the logical, scientific sphere, could not continue. A series of letters to Russell in February and March of 1914 indicates that Wittgenstein had made the transition to the identity-defining orientation of individuative-reflective faith.

> My letter must have shown you how totally different our ideas are, e.g., of the value of scientific work. . . . There can not be any real relation of friendship between us. I shall be grateful to you and devoted to you with all my heart for the whole of my life, but I shall not write to you again and you will not see me again either.[9]

Russell replied with such a nice letter that Wittgenstein felt compelled to restate his position:

> Our quarrels don't raise *just* from external reasons such as nervousness or over-tiredness but are—at any rate on *my* side—*very* deep-rooted. You may be right in saying that *we ourselves* are not *so very* different, but *our ideals* could not be more so. And that's why we haven't been able and we shan't *ever* be able to talk about anything involving our value-judgments without either becoming hypocritical or falling out. . . . Now perhaps, you'll say, "Things have more or less worked, up to the present. Why not go on in the same way?" But I'm *too* tired of this constant sordid compromise. My life has been one nasty mess so far—but need that go on indefinitely? . . . Let's write to each other about our work, our health, and the like, but let's avoid in our communications any kind of value-judgment, on any subject whatso-

ever, and let's recognize clearly that in such judgments neither of us could be *completely* honest without hurting the other. . . . I don't need to assure you of my deep affection for you, *but that affection would be in great danger if we were to continue with a relationship based on hypocrisy and for that reason a source of shame to us both.*[10]

Wittgenstein recognized that he and Russell held entirely different world views. Logic was more central to Russell's than to Wittgenstein's. Because he felt this distinction so much more sharply now that he was completing a new synthesis, Wittgenstein felt that the difference made it necessary to break off relations with those whose views were uncongenial to that synthesis.

In later recollections, Russell reflects on this dramatic change in Wittgenstein:

He was in the days before 1914 concerned almost solely with logic. During, or perhaps just before, the last war, he changed his outlook and became more or less of a mystic, as may be seen here and there in the *Tractatus.*[11]

Understood in the context of Wittgenstein's personal struggles, it would be more accurate to say that before 1914 Wittgenstein had radically separated logic from his interests in religious and ethical issues. He did not, in some mystical conversion experience, suddenly become interested in ethical issues in 1914; he did find that he could no longer keep those ethical concerns isolated from his studies of logic, mathematics, and science. In this new faith perspective—what Russell calls being a "mystic"—Wittgenstein sensed a need for finding a place in his developing philosophy for both logic and value. In July 1914, Wittgenstein expressed this concern to Russell:

I can't write you anything about logic today. Perhaps you regard this thinking about myself as a waste of time—but how can I be a logician before I'm a human being! *Far* the most important thing is to settle accounts with myself![12]

The Tractatus

In 1914, Wittgenstein returned to Vienna and joined the Austrian army. Although he had been working on the issues dealt with in the *Tractatus* since 1912, he did the actual writing while on active duty in the army. It is characteristic that even while in the army, Wittgenstein saw himself as a philosopher, not as a soldier. To understand Wittgenstein properly, it is necessary to understand his strong commitment to his profession. Philosophy for Wittgenstein was more than an occupation, it was "a consuming passion"; and not just *a* passion, but the only possible form of his existence; the thought of losing his gift for philosophy made him feel suicidal.[13] He held those philosophers in contempt who seemed to be halfheartedly involved with their work. Russell, in his *Autobiography,* says that his most tiring experience was arguing with Wittgenstein; Wittgenstein demanded total involvement in the philosophical dialogue.

Wittgenstein once remarked that he always felt as though he lived on the border line of insanity. He approached the task of philosophy with such commitment that he seemed to carry the problems of philosophy inside himself. This urgency allowed him to embody great creativity, but it also forced him to experience deep and recurring anxiety. Erich Heller (a student of Wittgenstein and an interpreter of his work) used lines by Friedrich Hebbel to describe Wittgenstein's passionate engagement with his work: "The hell fire of life consumes only the select among men. The rest stand in front of it, warming their hands."[14] Because of the intense involvement of the man in his work, it is necessary to deal with Wittgenstein's work to understand the development of his life.

Wittgenstein's philosophy has usually been divided into two major periods, *Tractatus Logico-Philosophicus* being representative of the first, and *Philosophical Investigations* of the second. Because these two works are very different, *Investigations* seeming to refute *Tractatus*, Wittgenstein is often credited with the founding of two different schools of philosophy. *Tractatus*, through its appropriation and interpretation by the Vienna Circle, became the foundation for logical positivism. *Philosophical Investigations* initiated the linguistic analysis movement, a philosophical methodology popular in England and America, which holds that many traditional philosophical problems can be resolved by attending to the language in which they are formulated and through which they are communicated. Neither logical positivism nor linguistic analysis seems to reflect Wittgenstein's profound sense of the seriousnes of philosophical problems of space, time, and deity.[15]

The *Tractatus* has generated misunderstanding. It is a short, concise, aphoristic work, difficult to comprehend in itself. Moreover, it was published in England for readers unfamiliar with the Viennese context in which its concerns were shaped. Finally, it was published with an introduction by Russell that Wittgenstein considered rejecting, feeling that it distorted the meanings of his work.

To understand Wittgenstein's intentions for the book, we must look briefly at the Viennese setting from which he came. At the turn of the century, Habsburg society was plagued with problems of poor housing, inadequate sanitation, and underpaid labor. The Empire ignored these social problems and rested on its grandeur and on the illusion of power founded more on its long history than on real social strength. Janik and Toulmin give succinct characterization of the prewar Habsburg Empire:

> The sensuous worldly splendor and glory apparent on its
> surface were, at a deeper level, the very same things that

were its misery. The stability of its society, with its delight in pomp and circumstance, was one expression of a petrified formality which was barely capable of disguising the cultural chaos that lay beneath it. On closer scrutiny, all its surface glories turned to their opposite; this is the fundamental truth about all aspects of life in the Dual Monarchy. These same paradoxes were reflected equally in its politics and its mores, its music and its press, its imperial aristocracy and its workers.[16]

Attempts to mask the dark realities of the culture behind the facade of past glory resulted in a falsification of all modes of expression. Political doubletalk corrupted communication, and there were no channels under the autocratic reign of Emperor Francis Joseph for effective political and social reform. All the normal drives toward reform were subverted, leaving only intellectual and artistic critiques of the society, without chance for real transformation.

In ways most of his interpreters fail to understand, Wittgenstein was motivated by his observation of the distance between intellectual discourse and social reality. He thought it essential to provide a philosophical basis that would allow empirical investigation and ethical reflection to commune without the reduction of both to impotence.

It seemed obvious to Wittgenstein that factual statements differ from ethical statements, and he believed that, using the logic of Russell and Frege, he could show each of these two necessary kinds of statements could be communicated in ways proper to their content. Because they did not understand this broader context for Wittgenstein's work, Russell and other English critics misinterpreted his work.

Wittgenstein actually approached this central philosophical problem by making a critique of language from within. He assumed that in order to talk about the world, there must be correspondence between language and reality. He developed on the basis of the logical theories of Russell and Frege a way of conceiving the relation between language and reality which would keep the ethical realm separate from the realm of sense data. Thinking that reality and language have correspondent structures, Wittgenstein articulated a "picture theory" of representation. Language pictures reality; if one understands the logical structures of language, one will at the same time be able to speak clearly and objectively about reality.

It is important to note that Wittgenstein thought that all complex propositions can be broken down into elementary propositions, each elementary proposition mirroring a fact, a "state of affairs." Only "states of affairs," empirical data, can be stated directly in language; causal or teleological relations between the facts cannot be directly stated because they transcend the states of affairs.

Although it is not possible to deal with causal or teleological relations directly, it is possible to use language to indicate those relationships.

> My propositions serve as elucidations in the following way: anyone who understands me eventually recognizes them as nonsensical, when he has used them—as steps—to climb up beyond them. (He must, so to speak, throw away the ladder after he has climbed up it.) He must transcend the world aright.[17]

Wittgenstein's theory of logic was adopted by the logical positivists who, combining it with their own empiricism, used it to support their claims that metaphysical, ethical, and religious statements are meaningless. According to them, and opposed to Wittgenstein himself, what cannot be directly stated cannot be said at all.

Wittgenstein met several times with members of the Vienna Circle, and he disagreed with their interpretations of his work. Much to their consternation, he would never refute them directly but insisted on reading them poetry by Tagore. His subtlety was lost on them. Over against all contrary interpretations, Wittgenstein believed that those things that cannot be directly stated are even more important than the facts that can be directly stated:

> The truth of the thoughts that are here communicated seems to me unassailable and definitive. I therefore believe myself to have found, on all essential points the final solution of the problems. And if I am not mistaken in this belief, then the second thing in which the value of this work consists is that it shows how little is achieved when these problems are solved.[18]

Letters written by Wittgenstein further precluded the possibility of accurately describing his work as positivist:

> *The book's point is an ethical one.* I once meant to include in the preface a sentence which is not in fact there now, but which I will write out for you here, because it will perhaps be a key to the work for you. What I meant to write, then, was this: My work consists of two parts: the one presented here plus all that I have *not* written. And *it is precisely this second part that is the important one.* My book draws limits to the sphere of the ethical from the inside as it were, and I am convinced that this is the ONLY rigorous way of drawing those limits.
>
> In short, I believe that where *many* others today are just *gassing,* I have managed in my book to put everything firmly into place by being silent about it. . . . For now I would recommend you to read the *preface* and the *conclusion* because they contain the most direct expression of the point of the book.[19]

Wittgenstein's position—that both science and ethics are valid, but that ethics can be communicated only indirectly, as in fable, music, or poetry—rests upon a world view in which sharp boundaries are drawn between fact and value. For Wittgenstein, this world view was absolute. It was the structure of his own faith-knowing that allowed him so forcefully to present an absolutist philosophical work designed to meet the needs of the culture of Vienna.

The Asceticism of Secular Sainthood

The *Tractatus* must be understood as a particular current in the flux of Wittgenstein's development. Even while he was finishing the work, he was going through profound changes. Although he never discussed his combat experiences with his friends, the war had a strong impact on his personality; he returned from the war with a much gloomier outlook than he had before, often expressing the opinion that humankind was doomed.

During this period of flux and gloom, Wittgenstein found in Tolstoy a figure who embodied the attitudes he had been trying to articulate in the *Tractatus*. He first began to admire Tolstoy when he read about him in James' *Varieties of Religious Experience*. In reading James' description of Tolstoy, it seems possible to speculate that one of the reasons that Wittgenstein so admired him was that they shared a common melancholia.

[Tolstoy's melancholy] . . . was logically called for by the clash between his inner character and his outer activities and aims. . . . Tolstoy was one of those primitive oaks of men to whom the superfluities and insincerities, the cupidities, complications, and cruelties of our polite civilization are profoundly unsatisfying, and for whom the eternal veracities lie with more natural and animal things. His crisis was the getting of his soul in order, the discovery of its genuine habitat and vocation, the escape from falsehoods into what for him were ways of truth. And though not many of us can imitate Tolstoy, not having enough, perhaps, of the aboriginal human marrow in our bones, most of us may at least feel as if it might be better for us if we could.[20]

Wittgenstein's appropriation of Tolstoy enabled him to harmonize his own life with the intellectual world view he had developed. Admiring Tolstoy's absolutist ethic, totally unsupported by intellectual assertions, Wittgenstein felt that he had found ways to live out an affirmation of both science and ethics which he had so recently worked out in theory.

When he returned to Vienna in 1918, Wittgenstein began immediately to alter his life-style. He walked into the bank and announced that he no longer wished to be encumbered by his fortune, nor to be befriended because of it. Because the sum was at least two million dollars, the bank contacted his family about his crazed behavior. The family decided that Wittgenstein's sisters would keep his money, with the understanding that they would return it to him when he came to his senses. Since he never attempted to reclaim his inheritance, it was eventually parceled out to various nieces and nephews.

At the same time he was renouncing his wealth, he made other alterations in living habits. He adopted an informal mode of dressing; he lived simply, even poorly, with very little furniture and no ornamentation; his meals often consisted only of oatmeal or powdered eggs, which he fixed for himself in his room.

Despite this new asceticism, he could not eliminate his sexual activities, and he despised himself for continuing them. He refused to escape his despairing predicament by accepting any theology of grace:

> I am clear about one thing: I am far too bad to be able to theorize about myself; in fact I shall either remain a swine or else I shall improve, and that's that! Only let's cut out the transcendental twaddle when the whole thing is as plain as a sock on the jaw.[21]

Since he sincerely believed that he was finished with philosophy on completion of the *Tractatus,* he felt that he needed to find a new career. During the first year after the war, Wittgenstein enrolled in a teacher-training program—with the strong support of his family, who thought he needed it more for therapy than for career preparation. He did not, however, find the program to be a pleasant experience, mainly because he could never overcome his feeling ridiculous attending classes with students considerably younger than himself.[22]

Worsening his already deep depression, he learned that David Pinsent, whom he claimed as his closest friend and to whom he had dedicated the *Tractatus,* had died in the war. In a letter to Russell, Wittgenstein wrote of his feelings about Pinsent's death: "Every day I think of Pinsent. He took half my life away with him. The devil will take the other half."[23]

Wittgenstein was also distressed over the rather poor reception the *Tractatus* was receiving. His ordeal was especially difficult because of the intensity with which his life and work had been bound together. By this time three of his brothers had committed suicide.[24]

Wittgenstein did somehow complete the teacher-training program despite his depression, and he took a job as schoolmaster in a small Austrian village—the first of three small villages in which he would serve in the period from 1920 to 1926. When he started work, he was enthusiastic about the possibility of helping the Austrian peasants, repeatedly telling friends that his aim was "to get the peasantry out of the muck."[25] The romantic ideals he held about the peasantry—ideals he had absorbed from Tolstoy—were soon to fade. After only a month in their midst, he described himself as surrounded by "odiousness and baseness."[26] This new way of feeling about the people among whom he worked proved more lasting than his earlier romantic notions; several years later, in a letter to Engelmann, he wrote that they were "not human at all but loathsome worms."[27] While he seemed to retain a sincere desire to reform his village charges, he never overcame his own preference for the company of cultured and well-educated people.

It is likely that the peasants easily sensed condescension in his attempts to reform them since it was so thinly veiled. He did not hesitate to make it known to them that he came from a wealthy Viennese family and that he had written a philosophical work that none of them would ever be able to understand. His ostentatious poverty naturally alienated villagers, and his responses to their concerns never served to mitigate their distrust. This is clearly illustrated by his response to a question about his religion.

> Wittgenstein replied that although he was not a Christian, he was an "evangelist". The villager was bewildered, for Wittgenstein emphasized that he did not mean that he was a Protestant (or "Evangelical"). . . . It appears he intended to suggest that although his business had something to do with the saving of souls and the proclamation of a gospel, these need not take place in a formal Christian framework.[28]

Despite the great chasm between Wittgenstein and the peasants, they did sometimes respond favorably to his efforts to help them. Occasionally he would take his pupils on trips to Vienna to widen their horizons; at such times, he would subsidize their expenses. When he came back from visits into the city, he would often bring fruit and chocolate to the children, who never got enough to eat. He would spend long hours after classes tutoring promising students, and he even attempted to arrange further schooling for a few of the boys. The villagers were not really comfortable with him, however, and often his efforts were rebuffed; many of them were afraid of having their children spend much time with an eccentric who was known to be homosexual. This aside, they wanted their children to stay on the farm and did not respond well to efforts to pull them away into the larger society.

The Passion of Serious Games

Wittgenstein did not get the peasants out of the muck, but his six years were not wasted. During this time, the seeds were being sown for his later philosophical work. Daily contact with children—giving him firsthand opportunity to observe how persons learn language—undermined some of his former beliefs in the logic of language. The metaphysical underpinnings to his philosophy, which he had expressed in the *Tractatus*, were gradually being worn away. After irreconcilable conflict with the villagers in 1926, Wittgenstein returned to Vienna, giving up his occupation as schoolmaster.

By this time, in 1926, the *Tractatus* had been discovered by wider philosophical circles and had become quite influential. Wittgenstein began constantly to receive requests to return to his work. He refused all offers, however, feeling incapable of doing creative philosophical work.

During the summer of 1926, right after resigning his post as schoolmaster, Wittgenstein went to work as a gardener at a monastery near Vienna. For a while he seriously contemplated becoming a monk. Not yielding to the temptation, he next worked for two years as an architect with his friend Engelmann; during this time he designed a home for his sister, Margarete Stoneborough. "His time as an architect prepared him psychologically, if in no other way, for his eventual decision to return to philosophy and to Cambridge in January, 1929."[29]

The stage theory of faith development helps to clarify what was happening during this period in Wittgenstein's life. His years as a schoolteacher must be understood not as a detour into irrelevancy, but as a reflection of his inner struggle to conform his life-style to the views expressed in the *Tractatus*. While he was living and working in the small towns, his need to isolate himself in order to pursue his ethical ideals gradually diminished. He began to doubt that the absolutist position he had expressed in the *Tractatus,* and had tried to live out in his work as schoolmaster, was truly a formulation of final truth.

In his struggles during the 1920s, his outlook was changing and new tensions were rising which eventually would lead to the coalescing of his entire life into a new orientation. His return to Cambridge in 1929 marks his affective transformation to the new worldview that had been in the making during the years after the war. It would be a mistake to suppose that this move marks the last change in his life; a development in content can be seen when one examines the *Blue* and *Brown Books* over against his *Philosophical Investigations.* Nevertheless, this new orientation that is reflected in his return to Cambridge and to philosophy does represent a move to what can be described as Wittgenstein's final stage of development.

Philosophical Investigations, the major work of this final period, was written over a fifteen-year span. The work is difficult to summarize because it presents a method of doing philosophy rather than a particular philosophical theory. In the book, there are 784 questions; 110 of these are answered, and 70 of the answers given are intended to be wrong answers.[30] The style of the work itself stands in sharp contrast to the style of the *Tractatus* and reflects an orientation that is much less absolutist than the claims of the *Tractatus.*

Although Wittgenstein in his second major work was concerned with many of the same issues that concerned him in the first, he did not attempt to present neat, simple solutions as he had done in the previous work. Wittgenstein no longer needed to affirm a logical framework that would provide ideological certainty to his view of reality. This time he developed the idea of various language-games and different possible forms of life in which language might be embedded and receive its meaning. He no longer thought that a logically structured language presented a single reality, but allowed that reality has many dimensions. In this conviction, marking his new stage of faith-knowing, Wittgenstein relinquished his previous absolutist world view for a view of the world which allowed for the existence and validity of many different approaches to reality. In his notion of many possible forms of life is the implicit recognition of the possible truth of positions which develop out of forms of life different from his own.

In this work, and in his life at this time, Wittgenstein displayed the characteristic paradoxical-consolidative ability to see the points of view of other persons or groups, and to see their world views from their perspectives. He never resolved the tension that is operative in this faith-knowing; this is suggested in his attitude toward religious symbols. Previously, when he supported his belief in the distinction between fact and value with a rigid world view, his schema had led him to regard religious language as attempts to say what cannot be said. With his new perspectives, religious language could be viewed as meaningful within a particular language-game. He now acknowledged the validity of other people's uses of religious symbols. For instance, during this period an old man told Wittgenstein that Jesus Christ was the world's greatest philosopher. "Wittgenstein tried to explain to him that Jesus Christ was not a philosopher at all; but he said afterwards that he understood why the old man wanted Christ to be the greatest of everything."[31] A few years earlier, he would not have been nearly so tolerant of others' attempts to express verbally those truths he thought were beyond direct speech.

Wittgenstein did often refer to the Last Judgment, which he found to be a powerful symbol, but he still considered much of the claims of theology and ethics to be incomprehensible. He could understand the notion of a

God who judges and redeems, but he found unintelligible the conception of God as a cosmological being who is characterized as the Creator of the world. Students' notes from seminars on the topic show that he struggled with the meaning of religious language; Norman Malcolm suggests that Wittgenstein did have real insight into the intent of religious symbol and language:

> When I once quoted to him a remark of Kierkegaard's to this effect: "How can it be that Christ does not exist, since I know that He has saved me?", Wittgenstein exclaimed: You see! It isn't a question of *proving* anything![32]

Wittgenstein considered Kierkegaard to have been the greatest philosopher of the nineteenth century. Malcolm says that Wittgenstein referred to Kierkegaard, "with something of awe in his expression, as a 'really religious' man."[33]

Wittgenstein continued to regard fables, poetry, and the theater as the best vehicles for communicating the mystical realm. He loved to attend American Western films, which he thought functioned as modern fable. He believed that all art should follow this cowboy-movie pattern—happy endings with the "good guys" victorious—or else it lacked the ethical message that, for him, was a necessary criterion of true art.

In 1947, Wittgenstein gave up his chair in philosophy at Cambridge and spent time afterward in Ireland, working on the last parts of the *Investigations*. In 1950 it was discovered that he had cancer, and he died in England in 1951, at the age of sixty-one. His last words were, "Tell them I've had a wonderful life."[34]

Many who knew him found this last statement perplexing because, from their perspective, his life had been so difficult and unhappy; the words are more comprehensible if one keeps in mind the complexity of Wittgenstein's character, in which a trusting, faithlike stance intertwined with a suspicious, skeptical outlook. Occasionally he displayed a faith that seemed uncharacteristic in light of his more generally pessimistic temperament; that "uncharacteristic" faith was likely what prevented him from fulfilling threats of suicide.

Throughout his life Wittgenstein displayed this vacillation between a doubting and trusting orientation to life. Interpreting Wittgenstein's life in terms of the faith–stage theory does not allow us to view his life as constant, progressive development of ever-deepening faith; it does allow us to see a developmental pattern in the way Wittgenstein dealt with these differing orientations both in his personal life and in his philosophical writings.

If we understand Wittgenstein's developing work as a correlate of his developing faith structures, we are able to see important continuities between his early work and his later work, continuities often obscured by examining the works individually and in isolation from the life of the man. In Wittgenstein, life and work are united in signal fashion.

Introduction

Seven years after World War II, students of theology received a remarkable legacy from a German pastor and scholar who died at the hands of the Nazis just before the end of the war in 1945. A slim volume of Dietrich Bonhoeffer's *Letters and Papers from Prison* introduced the world to a "religionless" interpretation of Christianity, not a creed built on the traditions and dogmas of the church, but a faith in Jesus Christ, the "man for others" who points the way to a new style of life that is fully engaged with the needs of the world.

While these ideas were no surprise to the close friends who had followed Bonhoeffer's thinking and shared his resistance to Hitler's power in Germany, theologians elsewhere in Europe and in America were left struggling to relate this new vision to the young theologian they had known before the war, so ardent in his loyalty to the church and so carefully, thoughtfully orthodox in his theology. The distance between the pastor who planned a trip to India to study Gandhi's philosophy of nonviolence and the intelligence agent who waited out the anxious hours while his colleagues planted a bomb that was supposed to take *Der Fuehrer's* life seemed to many a gulf too wide to cross. Yet there was no mistake; Bonhoeffer had made that journey himself, and he retained all the way the remarkable seriousness of purpose, sense of humor, and love of companionship that characterized his unique personality.

Today, thirty-five years after his death, serious questions about his faith still invite exploration. Did Bonhoeffer really create a new model for the life and ministry of the church, or was he merely voicing his dissatisfaction with the timidity of his churchly colleagues in the face of Nazi tyranny? Was the plot against Hitler an act of Christian discipleship or a mistaken alliance with the forces of violence? Is the "religionless" interpretation of Christianity Bonhoeffer's denial of his earlier faith, or his recovery of a genuine relationship to God?

In this essay, Robin W. Lovin, who teaches religious ethics at the University of Chicago, and Jonathan P. Gosser, who is a United Methodist pastor and a graduate student at the University of Notre Dame, apply the resources of faith development theory to the task of understanding the transformations and the continuity in Bonhoeffer's faith.

Dietrich Bonhoeffer:
Witness in an Ambiguous World

Robin W. Lovin and Jonathan P. Gosser

Dietrich Bonhoeffer is surrounded by a nimbus of mystery. Thirty years after his death, his theology remains the topic of lively debate among scholars, and his vision of a renewed church living Christ's life for others expresses the hopes of serious Christians around the world. Yet the questions about his own faith, which were provoked by the first fragmentary publication of his prison letters, remain unresolved, despite the appearance of his *Gesammelte Schriften,* a definitive biography, and an immense body of secondary literature.[1] The corpus of Bonhoeffer's theology is available for study, the lines of influence on his thinking have been traced; yet, the man himself remains elusive.

In large measure, he would have wanted it so. His christocentric theology demands a disciplined surrender of self and a restraint of all that is idiosyncratic, so that the living Word of God may be heard through the human voice and the presence of Christ may be felt in the human presence. This theological discipline, moreover, coincides in Bonhoeffer with a certain aristocratic reserve, a reluctance to put oneself forward or to cheapen one's sensitivities by displaying them in public. There are no motion pictures of Bonhoeffer and no recordings of his voice. He was seldom photographed except in groups, and there are few manuscripts in which the man intrudes unprotected and unreserved, even on the private pages of his own writings.

A biographical sketch of Dietrich Bonhoeffer, especially one exploring the development of his personal faith, is a project that would be uncongenial to the subject. Nevertheless, it is a necessary project. It is only as the man emerges for us from his work that we are restrained from appropriating his suggestive, enigmatic, and fragmentary words and twisting them entirely to our own purposes. It is only when we can first hear Bonhoeffer—and not merely the echo of our own thoughts—that we have a chance to hear through him the living Word that he would have us believe confronts us in this, our own time.

In these pages, then, we will try to illuminate some key moments in Bonhoeffer's personal history. These may not be the moments that were most memorable to him, or the most dramatic, or the most important for the future of the church and its theology. They are, rather, the moments that open for us the structure of his faith and show us that structure in the process of transformation.

A Secure Foundation

A child reacts to the conditions of life even before it is aware of itself as a distinct person and before it can imagine alternatives to its present discomfort or joy. Thus the preconditions of faith are set before a child makes any conscious decisions or has any awareness of "religious" questions and problems. A faith that is to grow requires a prelinguistic, preconceptual foundation in love, trust, and security. Dietrich Bonhoeffer was born into a family that provided these abundantly.

On February 4, 1906, Paula Bonhoeffer gave birth to twins—a boy and a girl. She and her husband, Karl, had five older children; the newborns, Dietrich and Sabine, joined Karl, Walter, Klaus, Ursula, and Christine. A younger sister, Susanne, was born in 1909.

The twins were born into a home already well ordered to meet the needs of five active children. Paula Bonhoeffer, a woman of extensive education and aristocratic ancestry, managed the large household with grace and efficiency, first in the Silesian city of Breslau, where her husband held a professorship in psychiatry, and then in Berlin after Karl joined the faculty of the University there in 1912. Thus, Dietrich's childhood belongs to that now-vanished world of enormous rooms filled with family portraits, Mozart in the evenings, country houses in the summer, and an ample staff of servants to maintain the standards this life-style required.

Karl Bonhoeffer demanded intellectual honesty and precision from his children, and under his influence they grew to dread cliches and hollow phrases. His dinner table inquiries into the children's activities and opinions set a standard of achievement and self-discipline that awed the neighbor children and, later Dietrich's fellow students.

The children themselves, however, remembered their family home as a place of love, and it kept a central place in all their lives even after they reached adulthood. Parental discipline was balanced by a sensitive adjustment of household arrangements both to meet the children's real needs and to challenge their abilities. Karl Bonhoeffer, his daughter Christine wrote, "was not the kind of father whose beard one would stroke or whom one could call by a pet name, but when he was needed, he was firm as a rock. And how he always knew where the shoe pinched is a mystery to me to this day."[2]

Thus life in the Bonhoeffer family provided from the beginning an atmosphere of trust and warmth, which was important for all that was to follow in Dietrich's life. One follows the career of Bonhoeffer the student, the pastor, the lecturer with a sense that this was a young man with the wind always at his back. His intense concentration, his interest in people, his ability to handle prodigious amounts of both work and play made him the wonder of his colleagues. He had the manners and the interests typical of his comfortable, aristocratic background, but his intensity and energy were fed by the deeper sense of security that emerged from the trustworthy environment of the Bonhoeffer family home.

The Singer of Songs

The active, constructive stages of faith development begin when a child first appropriates the values and symbols that appear in this early nurturing environment. What is important, what is trustworthy, what is approved and desired is communicated in words, moods, and actions by the parents. The child enters into this adult world in an episodic and fantasy-filled way, appropriating ideas and images that will be the building blocks for his own coherent world view.

For Dietrich, the materials for this appropriation came almost exclusively from the family. The household itself, with loving, capable, and interested parents, a governess to look after one's needs, and older brothers to admire and to imitate, provided virtually all the resources the boy could need for play or education.

Religious life, in particular, was the province of Dietrich's mother. The Bonhoeffer family rarely attended public worship, but Paula Bonhoeffer, the daughter and granddaughter of theologians, took her Protestant faith seriously. The children said their prayers at bedtime, and their mother planned elaborate rituals for Christmas and New Year's Eve—events that always remained vivid in the children's memories. Karl Bonhoeffer held a skeptical attitude toward theology and the church, but he participated readily in his wife's plans, and Dietrich seems to have been unaware until later that his father and older brothers had reservations about religion. When Dietrich and Sabine were old enough to begin lessons at home they were entrusted to a tutor, but their mother retained the religious instruction for herself.

The content of Dietrich's family faith was thus a liberal Protestant version of God and Jesus, based on Bible stories and familiar hymns. However, Dietrich's appropriation of this faith was by no means confined to the public setting of family rituals. From an early age he was engaged in a deeply personal shaping and testing of his faith, an enterprise that he pursued with the same energy and devotion that would later characterize his work as a theologian. The puzzle of death seems to have been central to these early reflections. Before the family moved to Berlin, the children sometimes watched events in a cemetery near their home, so that they had an early exposure to death and mourning. At the age of seven, Dietrich experienced the accidental death of a playmate, and by 1915 World War I was bringing the first reports of casualties among the family and friends. As the boy's cognitive capacities grew, he continually tried to fit these events into his developing understanding of the world. Sabine tells the story of one spiritual exploration, which was shared by both of the twins:

> From eight to ten years old Dietrich and I slept in the same room, and when we were in bed at night, we used to have earnest discussions about death and life. The war of 1914 had broken out and we heard of the deaths of our big cousins and some of the fathers of our classmates. And so in the evenings after prayers and hymn singing . . . we used to lie awake for a long time and try to imagine what it must be like to be dead and to have entered upon eternal life. We used to make special efforts to draw nearer every evening to eternity by resolving to think only of the word "eternity" and not to

admit any other thought to our minds. This eternity seemed to us very long and uncanny. . . . We staunchly kept up this self-imposed exercise for a long time.[3]

The faith that Dietrich was exploring was soon tested by a crisis that disrupted the supportive family milieu. Karl-Friedrich and Walter, the oldest of the Bonhoeffer sons, were called to military service in 1917. Walter was wounded shortly after his arrival at the front, and he died a few days later. The effect on Paula Bonhoeffer was shattering. She spent several weeks in almost complete isolation, and her careful provisions for the family's life together were suspended for some time thereafter. Thus the eleven-year-old Dietrich had to carry his own intense grief without the loving support he had always known in the past.

Dietrich's parents' sorrow was compounded by the awareness that Walter had not received adequate medical care in the field hospital at the front. What was unbearable was not so much the loss of their son as the knowledge that they could perhaps have saved him. Travel to the front was almost impossible for civilians, but a man of Professor Bonhoeffer's standing would no doubt have been able to arrange the journey to bring his son home for competent attention to his wounds. The hesitation to use the privileges of rank, the decision to share their misfortune with all the other parents of lesser means, was entirely characteristic of Karl and Paula Bonhoeffer, but it cost them bitterly. Tragedy could be borne, but the failure to have done everything one could was almost enough to break the spirit.[4]

How to relate this early experience of insecurity and loss to Bonhoeffer's faith development remains something of a puzzle, primarily because his own thoughts at the time are unknown. The sense he made of this family tragedy perhaps comes clear during the Second World War, when

Dietrich decided in the end to use his family connections to secure an assignment that would exempt him from the military call-up. The lesson learned in 1918 may have been articulated only much later, in a letter from Tegel in December of 1943:

> The past weeks have been more of a strain than anything before that. There's no changing it, only it's more difficult to adapt oneself to something that one thinks could have been prevented than to something inevitable. But when facts have taken shape, one just has to fit in with them. . . . I now think that we ought first of all to do everything we can to change those facts while there's still time; and then, if we've tried everything, even though it has been in vain, they will be much easier to bear.[5]

More influential even than these tragic events on Dietrich's further development was his discovery of the joys of music. Just at the time that events were shaking the emotional solidarity of the Bonhoeffer household, Dietrich was developing real competence in one of the family's unifying activities—an activity that undergirded the family's times of faith and celebration and one that even his father and the skeptical older brothers enjoyed.

It is not surprising that an educated and aristocratic family, familiar with the cultural life of the German capital, should have well-developed tastes and a keen critical sense for the arts, but it is apparent that members of this family pursued these topics not only with discrimination, but with genuine enjoyment and personal satisfaction. Music, particularly, seems to have provided an important cement in the family fellowship. It provided, first, a place for the Bonhoeffer children to demonstrate their abilities and their diligence, and then, later, it was a common ground on which the Bonhoeffers could come together for a respite from their specialized pursuits.

Throughout Dietrich Bonhoeffer's life, this fellowship was an important center of meaning and loyalty. We have early glimpses of him accompanying his mother's songs on the piano or arranging pieces for himself; and just before his arrest in 1943, he joined the family in singing Walcha's *Lobe den Herren* for his father's seventy-fifth birthday.

Bonhoeffer's early interest in music should be noted carefully by serious students of his theology. The picture of the budding musician and singer provides, of course, an important counterbalance to the image of a rather withdrawn and introspective youth which we may see if we are looking only at the meditations on death and eternity that presage the appearance of a theologian; but more than that, we suggest that the roots of the theologian are here, too, in the fellowship and the music. Bonhoeffer's theology of Christ existing as community derives biographically from real experience of fellowship, not from academic exposure to the sociologists' abstraction, "community."[6] In music itself, Bonhoeffer found perhaps his earliest model for the order and wholeness that he later sought to explicate in theology. For a child concerned to grasp the order of things, to find a system of symbols that is both expressive and concrete, music is a mythic world complete in itself. These moving and ethereal sounds, once their mysteries are understood, can be reduced to dots arranged on lines, reproduced from those same dots, even rearranged to produce new and pleasing forms when the dots are manipulated according to the rules.

We know that young Dietrich Bonhoeffer was a skillful pianist, so skillful that his parents thought he might become a concert artist. Doubtless he found in music one of the few activities that could satisfy both his father's critical standards and his mother's sensitiveness. He also found there an outlet for the powers of imagination and creativity that are the child's way of ordering and mastering his world.

DIETRICH BONHOEFFER

That Dietrich Bonhoeffer gave signs of becoming a musician in a family of doctors, lawyers, and scientists tells us something about the theologian he finally did become. By giving proper emphasis to these early artistic activities in Dietrich's religious development, we can see that from the beginning he sought meaning and order in a realm of shared, social activity, rather than in private, specialized investigations. Even his most personal reflections, as he recalled them in the later autobiographical fragments, are filled with a hunger to share his insights and to test his commitments. If that impulse was sometimes stifled by shyness, by reticence, or even by a youthful inability to articulate his insights with the precision his father would demand, there seems little doubt that the social impulse was, nonetheless, dominant—the *cantus firmus* of the boy's developing sense of the world's order and of his own place in it.

Music, too, provided his model of mastery in this world, for the competence he sought was not the mastery of technical skills or encyclopedic knowledge. The competence he sought was virtuosity, the combination of skill, knowledge, and timing in an apparently effortless performance that brings the elements together and makes them available to the hearer as they are needed. It is little wonder that this young man, like so many others of his generation, was attracted to the unrestrained, vigorous theology of Karl Barth, the theologian who loved Mozart and who submerged his massive erudition in a free and even playful service of the Word.

Finally, we should note that it was this social realm, with its distinctive forms of mastery, which early captured Dietrich's vocational interest. While the other Bonhoeffers dealt with music as a hobby, Dietrich's skill and interest suggested that it might be a career. "Thus in his boyhood and youth it was music that gave him a special position at school and among his fellow-students. This was granted to him by his brothers and sisters as well."[7] While the prospect of a concert career did not materialize, it remained true that the vocation Dietrich chose was to articulate and systematize the sense of the world as a locus for human community that was present, implicitly, in the activities and values that made his family's world. From the child who sang "Nun zu guter Letzt . . . " to his brother departing for the Western Front to the theologian who expressed without rationalization or self-justification the moral basis for the conspiracy against Hitler, Dietrich Bonhoeffer had as gift and as calling the expression of fundamental ideas that remained hidden or only self-expressed among his family and compatriots.

In this sense we may say that Bonhoeffer found his vocation long before he decided for theology. Music, as he experienced music in his family circle, became the paradigm for what it meant to have a world and to be at home in it. In this nexus of order, sociality and virtuosity, the mythic-literal imagination of childhood constructed its own careful appropriation of the world into which he was born and gave that paradigm a power and clarity that made it the developmental foundation for all that would follow, both in theology and in action.

His calling, alone among the Bonhoeffer brothers, was to appropriate the order that prevailed around the dinner table and in the sitting-room at 14 Wangenheimstrasse and to pursue it until it connected with an order of value and meaning in the world, an order permanent enough to withstand the shocks of experience and profound enough to absorb his attention throughout his life. What other men—the specialists in law or medicine or politics—might ruminate over on their beds at night and dismiss in their working hours with "I know nothing of such things," these things Dietrich Bonhoeffer made his life's work. To the task he brought his own resources of intellect and experience, and he performed his duties in a distinctive way, but he identified its origins in the fragment of a drama he wrote in Tegel: "I know the tranquil strength there is in a good bourgeoise home. No one can know that if they have not grown up in it."[8]

The Seeker of Experience

Dietrich apparently decided to become a theologian quite early, perhaps as early as the time of Walter's death, and certainly by 1920.[9] Thus his path was clear to him when he began his university studies at Tübingen in 1923 at the age of seventeen.

It was family tradition that the Bonhoeffer sons would begin their university studies at their father's alma mater, but Dietrich was the only one also to join his father's fraternity, the Igel ("Hedgehog"). Founded in 1871, it was an independent Swabian fraternity dedicated to the ideals of German political liberalism. Originally, the Igel had marked itself off in sharp distinction to the brightly bedecked dueling fraternities by its choice of shades of gray for its colors and a hedgehog skin for its emblem, but the Igel, too, succumbed to the enticements of nationalism and the pressures of nazification. The Igel adopted the anti-Semitic "Aryan clause" in 1933, and Dietrich resigned his membership soon afterward. While he was at Tübingen, however, he enjoyed the sense of solidarity with these contemporaries.

During the 1920s, the German army was limited by treaty to a strength of 100,000, but the government provided semi-secret military training for many young men, partly to provide a reserve force to counter any anti-Weimar rising by Communist or Nazi elements. (Hitler rose to prominence with his abortive "Beer Hall Putsch" in Munich in 1923.) Dietrich went with other members of his fraternity to take fourteen days of military training with the Ulm Rifles. His participation in this

"Black Reichswehr" seems to have been motivated by a desire to help the Igel provide its full complement of trainees, and a commitment to be helpful in the event of a crisis in the Republic, along with his continuing thirst for new experiences.[10]

The most lasting influence of the studies in Tübingen was doubtless the course of New Testament lectures offered by Adolf Schlatter during the summer term. Although Dietrich had little personal contact with Schlatter, his works became an essential part of the young theologian's working library, and later he would refer his own students to them.

In 1924, Dietrich visited Italy and North Africa with his brother Klaus, and in Rome among the crowds in St. Peter's during Holy Week he acquired his first positive impressions of Roman Catholicism. The experience shaped a vision of the Church for him which was thereafter always less exclusively Protestant than his family background might suggest. "Often during the celebrations in these mighty surroundings," he wrote, "the Protestant church seems like no more than a small sect."[11]

Early in his university studies, then, we find the young Bonhoeffer exploring the parameters of faith primarily through observing, comparing, and evaluating the conventional forms in which faith is lived in different places. This period of exploration inaugurated by the visit to Rome had a profound influence on his later writing. The influence is seen not so much in his theological ideas, for Dietrich was not seeking ideas at this time. He was seeking experiences, seeking to know, firsthand, the places and the actions in which people find meaning in their lives. What he learned in St. Peter's, and never forgot, was that the Church is one such source of meaning, that a Christian community has a value beyond the theology it produces or the personal piety it nurtures.

This insight took intellectual form in his subsequent

theological studies. Upon his return to Germany in 1924, he enrolled at the University of Berlin, and in 1927 he completed a doctoral thesis entitled *Sanctorum Communio, the Communion of Saints.* During the following years, he served as assistant pastor to a German congregation in Barcelona, Spain, and then returned to Berlin to prepare for work as a lecturer in the theological faculty.

For all his travel and study, Bonhoeffer's experience remained closely tied to his family and to German culture. This is hardly surprising, since the family was connected to the leading circles of science and politics, as well as art and theology, and the University of Berlin was one of the world's great intellectual centers at the time. All that even Dietrich Bonhoeffer's voracious intellectual appetite could consume was readily available to him within the family circle, or a few blocks away in Berlin.

Yet it is not surprising, either, that a young man of Bonhoeffer's boundless curiosity would also want to explore the world from a new perspective. From 1928 onward, he spoke often of a desire to visit India.[12] His first extensive experience outside of German culture and beyond the paths his family could readily mark for him came in the United States. In 1930 Bonhoeffer completed the requirements for appointment as a lecturer in theology, with the preparation of a manuscript titled *Act and Being.* No permanent post was available for the twenty-four-year-old scholar, however, so he accepted a fellowship at Union Theological Seminary in New York.[13]

Anticipating difficulties with language and hostility over Germany's role in World War I, he prepared himself for this adventure by compiling a notebook of American idioms and drafting answers to questions about Germany's war guilt. While the vocabulary no doubt proved useful, he shortly learned that the defense of his country was not usually needed, and he plunged at once into a range of experiences much wider than the discussions of theology and the Treaty of Versailles that he had expected.

From his base at Union Seminary, he traveled to Mexico and Cuba, and he established close friendships with other European students who helped to establish the ecumenical perspective of his future work. He met the French student Jean Lasserre, whose conversation moved him beyond his dissatisfaction with the Treaty of Versailles to a serious consideration of Christian pacifism. Here, too, he found a theological ally in the Swiss student, Erwin Sutz, who later arranged for Bonhoeffer's first personal contact with Karl Barth.

While establishing these European friendships and continuing his family's pattern of active concert and theater attendance, Dietrich also plunged into a serious study of the American religious scene. Paul Lehmann, an American who spoke fluent German, helped Bonhoeffer bridge the gap between German and American theology, but Dietrich remained skeptical of the American lack of concern with dogmatics and exegesis, which for him not only flawed the theology at Union but often spoiled the preaching at the churches he visited in midtown Manhattan.

The search for a more satisfying worship experience led him to Harlem, where his friend Albert "Frank" Fisher introduced him to the Abyssianian Baptist Church. Bonhoeffer and Fisher taught a Sunday school class there, and Dietrich often visited in the homes of the congregation. At this time, he began his record collection of Negro spirituals, particularly those recorded by Paul Robeson.

During the year at Union, Bonhoeffer, Lasserre, and Sutz—guided on the first leg of the trip by Paul Lehmann—set out to cross the United States and to visit Mexico in a decrepit Oldsmobile. The Oldsmobile survived the four-thousand-mile trip, though they chose to travel by train in Mexico; and Dietrich returned to New York with a rich experience of American life that widened his horizons far beyond any of the travels he had taken in Europe.

In a sense, Bonhoeffer's world in 1931 had expanded to its widest bounds. By then, he had not only completed his theological education with academic distinction; he had learned to explore freely the concrete varieties of faith that were available to him. Even the rich background of experience and opportunity offered by his family had been surpassed, and the young Berlin academic could now move in classrooms, churches, and homes far beyond the realms of the German intellectual elite.

Yet at just this point the search for experience reached its limits. Even as he continued to plan further explorations, agreeing to attend an ecumenical conference in England and investigating again the possibilities for a voyage to India, Bonhoeffer was dimly aware that to possess the world, even an extraordinarily large and varied world, was not enough. He needed also to locate himself within that world, to be an individual and to fix some loyalties to bind his own identity. This restless probing and testing—this search for a method, a milieu, or a teacher—existed in tension with a reluctance to make any commitments that might foreclose the search. Thus, Bonhoeffer quickly moved to test the new "crisis theology" of Karl Barth against the nervous liberalism of Berlin and the triumphant liberalism of New York, but he did not seek a personal encounter with Barth until after the American term of 1930-31. The outcome of that meeting was both exhilarating and disturbing. Immediately upon the event he wrote to Erwin Sutz: "I don't think I have ever regretted anything in my theological past as much as the fact that I did not come here earlier."[14]

Later in the year another thought intruded: "If once in my life I could have met up with an older man to work with, a man who would really have become my teacher!—I don't know why that should never happen to me. Or wouldn't I have been able to stand it?"[15]

One senses beneath the light tone of these letters to Sutz, Bonhoeffer's profound personal uneasiness. Yet, developmentally, this alternation between enthusiasm and withdrawal is precisely what we would expect from a young man who has established his autonomy and ability, but who has not yet quite completed the circle of explorations that must precede an authentic personal commitment.

The developmental perspective, then, suggests that Bonhoeffer the maturing scholar, the fledgling pastor, the neophyte lecturer, is best understood in all these roles as a seeker of experience. His faith is a synthetic-conventional faith. He draws meanings and values from an unusually rich and diverse mix of sources, to be sure, but he does not yet exhibit a personal commitment that knows the price of individuation and is prepared to pay it. Already in Bonhoeffer's earliest academic works, *Sanctorum Communio* and *Act and Being,* we see an early attempt at an individuative-reflective stance that would mark out an intellectual position distinctly his own; but we find in the letters to Sutz an awareness that this process of self-identification is still somehow incomplete. At this stage of development, vocational commitment was not a place to make a stand; it was a guide to exploration. Those who are called, as Bonhoeffer would be soon enough, to draw the dividing lines and speak the decisive word are fortunate indeed if, before that struggle, life provides them with the time and the resources to know the world before they are obliged to remake it. That was the opportunity that Dietrich Bonhoeffer enjoyed during the 1920s.

The Servant of the Church

In a sense Dietrich's decision to become a theologian had been quite fruitful. At the age of twenty-five, he had become a university lecturer, published two theological works, and was increasingly recognized in ecumenical circles. He had, indeed, become a theologian, as the other men in the Bonhoeffer family had become psychiatrists, lawyers, and physicists; and he had acquitted himself honorably.

However, this appropriation of theological and professional identity had been primarily an intellectual project, effected with a kind of mental exhilaration, but with little emotional turmoil. It was after the return from New York that the identity of the young scholar was first subjected to real tension. The Nazis were coming to power in Germany, and Bonhoeffer had concluded along with the rest of his family that this could only bring disaster. Two days after Hitler became Chancellor, Bonhoeffer delivered an address, "The Younger Generation's Changed View of the Concept of Leader (Fuehrer)," broadcast over Berlin radio. He was cut off the air before he finished.

Bonhoeffer's special concern for the victims of Hitler's actions, especially for the Jews who lost jobs and property because of the "Aryan Laws," quickly led him to the limits of his Lutheran convictions about the separation of the church from political life. The ministry of the church, he wrote in April of 1933, includes "an unconditional obligation to the victims of any ordering of society, even if they do not belong to the Christian community."[16]

This position was controversial in itself at a time when one church leader could speak of anti-Semitic violence as "justifiable collective anger."[17] Bonhoeffer, however, was prepared to go one step further. In extreme cases, the church may have a responsibility " . . . not just to bandage the victims under the wheel, but to put a spoke in the wheel itself."[18]

In this statement, Bonhoeffer was ahead of his church and perhaps even ahead of himself. His careful rehearsal of the rationale for direct Christian political action was not followed by active participation in the German resistance until 1940. Nevertheless, the theological guidelines for the path he would eventually follow were sketched in bold strokes early in the Nazi period.

The political challenge of Nazism came to Bonhoeffer on the heels of a profound personal transformation, a movement he described as a turn from "phraseology to reality." Eberhard Bethge, in his biography of Bonhoeffer, titles this period "The Theologian Becomes a Christian." In developmental terms, this crisis was a transition from a critical attitude of exploration to a stance of commitment, from learning to analyze, test, and compare the languages of various theological frameworks to taking a single position that defines one's identity and guides one's acceptance of responsibilities and risks.

Bonhoeffer endured this time of testing with his usual reticence. He retained the good humor that characterized him in all crises. What gave way, momentarily, was the consistency between life and thought that usually marked this man. While lecturing on the Creation at the university, he argued that the human condition was one of being "in the middle," from which one could know neither beginning nor ending. At the same time, privately, he was writing strangely romantic accounts of his childhood religion and of his decision to become a theologian.[19] The contradiction between his academic rejection of the search for beginnings—a search he labeled in his lectures as "systematic despair"[20]—and his private, literary re-creations of his origins marks a gap between theory and experience that is rarely found in Bonhoeffer's life.

This struggle left Bonhoeffer a changed person. Those who had known him before, especially his American friends, could not overlook the difference. Dietrich was now a serious churchman, not only a scholar; and he had adopted the practice of daily meditation on scripture which he would keep to the very end. Rarely, obliquely, he himself gave an account of the change that had taken place:

> Is it . . . intelligible to you if I say I am not at any point willing to sacrifice the Bible as the strange word of God, that on the contrary, I ask with all my strength what God is trying to say to us through it . . . ? Also I want to say to you quite personally that since I have learned to read the Bible in this way—and that does not date from such a very long time ago—it becomes more marvelous to me every day.[21]

The Bonhoeffer who emerged from this testing period is in many respects the model of the man of faith whose vision of the world encounters certain unavoidable polarities and who seeks the support of a disciplined community to champion a program of resolution. He was certainly the man for the time in which he lived, for his personal crisis prepared him for the German Church Struggle, and his new perspective allowed him to see more clearly what was ultimately at stake in what others at first perceived as minor issues. In the face of intellectual confusion or demonic certainty, he was among the first to draw a sharp distinction between Protestant Christianity and National Socialism, and to insist that one could not conflate them, but only choose between them. When others, reluctantly or eagerly, imagined an "evangelical Church that is rooted in our nationhood,"[22] Bonhoeffer spoke the word that drew the lines:

> It is becoming more and more clear to me that we are to be given a great national people's Church, whose nature will no longer be Christian, and that we must be prepared for the completely new paths we will then have to take. The question is really Germanism or Christianity, and the sooner the conflict comes into the open the better.[23]

In the face of this emerging crisis in the church, Bonhoeffer found the secure and independent identity that eluded him in the years of travel and academic success. He became the servant of his embattled church. In a letter written several years later, when he was director of a seminary of the Confessing Church at Finkenwalde, Dietrich reflected on his faith crisis and the decision to which it led him:

> Then something happened, something that has changed and transformed my life to the present day. For the first time I discovered the Bible. . . . I had often preached, I had seen a great deal of the Church, and talked and preached about it—but I had not yet become a Christian. . . .
> For all my abandonment, I was quite pleased with myself. Then the Bible, and in particular the Sermon on the Mount, freed me from that. Since then everything has changed. I have felt this plainly, and so have other people about me. It was a great liberation. It became clear to me that the life of a servant of Jesus Christ must belong to the Church, and step by step it became plainer to me how far that must go.
> Then came the crisis of 1933. This strengthened me in it. Also, I now found others who shared that aim with me. The revival of the Church and of the ministry became my supreme concern. . . .
> I must follow the path. Perhaps it will not be such a long one. Sometimes we wish that it were so (Philippians 1:23). But it is a fine thing to have realized my calling.[24]

Bonhoeffer's faith crisis led to the development of a heightened ability to view his world in terms of polarities and to draw sharp and unbending lines separating divergent points of view, and also in his own life to draw a sharp distinction between the state of his faith before and after he "discovered the Bible." But even more important, this new development in Bonhoeffer's faith coincided with the needs of the Church Struggle in Germany, and there, on the side of what was to become the Confessing Church,

Dietrich was able to live out his commitment to Christ as a servant of the church, and to find some "others who shared that aim" with him.

For Dietrich, this service was a total identity that left no room for ambiguity or divided commitments. It meant the investment of his scholarship, his penchant for travel, his good humor, his heightened ability to dichotomize, his ecumenical contacts—all these and more—in the struggle for integrity within the church. It led him to break off a promising relationship with a young woman to whom he wrote that letter from Finkenwalde, so that he might devote himself even more completely to the needs of the church. Before the end of his life, he would arrive at a new understanding of these personal commitments, but for now, "the life of a servant of Jesus Christ must belong to the Church."

In the years that followed, Dietrich Bonhoeffer became a spokesman for the "Confessing Church," the bold step a group of Christian leaders launched in opposition to the Nazification of all German institutions after 1933. When it was clear that the pro-Nazi "German Christians" would gain control of the Protestant churches of Germany and unite them in a single Reich Church under the domination of the state, the leaders of the opposition called for a renewed commitment to the historic confessional formulations of the Christian faith.

This church was not, in its conception, a sect or a denomination. Rather, the Confessing Church claimed that the Reich Church had forfeited its claim to preach the Word of God and that the Confessing Church was heir to the faith of the Reformation in Germany. The Confessing Church was not an alternative structure. It was, in the minds of its leaders, *the* church in Germany.

Bonhoeffer quickly became a leading spokesman for this claim. To do so made his position as a lecturer in Berlin untenable, so late in 1933 he accepted a call to serve two

German congregations in London. There he was free to pass information on the state of the church in Germany to leaders of the ecumenical movement and to use his pulpit in a foreign capital to arrange various embarrassments for the Reich Church and its leaders.

In 1935 the Confessing Church called Bonhoeffer to take charge of a seminary for its ordination candidates in Pomerania. The school soon settled on an estate at Finkenwalde, which served as the center of Bonhoeffer's work until the Gestapo closed the school in 1937.

Throughout this period, Bonhoeffer wanted to keep the boundaries of the Confessing Church sharp and clear. He resisted, even more than his compatriots, any cooperation that would imply a recognition of the Reich Church government, and he was instrumental in providing theological and confessional clarity for the Confessing Church. Especially at the beginning of the struggle, he looked to the Confessing Church synods as bodies empowered to speak an authoritative word to the churches, and he did not scruple to use his seminarians as a pressure group at these gatherings.

In 1936 Bonhoeffer published a paper, "On the Question of the Church Community," in which he defended the proposition, "Whoever knowingly separates himself from the Confessing Church in Germany cuts himself off from salvation."[25] The work caused a sensation at the time, but from our present distance we can see the paper as a coherent expression of his major concerns at the time. Bonhoeffer at this stage in his life structured his world in sharp dichotomies and demanded choices between the poles of experience—a clear manifestation of individuative-reflective faith. At this point his early concern for the church as a community, his interest in the Church of Rome, and his Protestant stress on individual affirmation all came together in support of a doctrine of the church that confronted each individual with a radical choice.

Bonhoeffer thus found himself increasingly isolated, not only from the pro-Nazi German Christian movement, but from others in his own Confessing Church who either hoped for conciliation or who were determined to avoid conflict with the state. In the end, not only was Bonhoeffer an irritant to the Reich's Church Affairs Office; he was alienated from many of his earlier companions in the Church Struggle.

It was during this period that the writings by which he became known to a wider public first appeared. *The Cost of Discipleship* worked out in detail the implications for Christian discipleship of the Sermon on the Mount, the very passage of Scripture that struck him so forcefully in his own faith crisis in 1932. *Life Together* was published as a report on the Finkenwalde experiment, with its discipline of study, worship, meditation, and active involvement in the Church Struggle.

In these two books we have Bonhoeffer's own theological reflections on the path he had taken since his personal crisis in 1932–33 and his prescription for the church he loved and whose servant he had determined to be.

The Servant of the World

As the diplomatic situation in Europe deteriorated and the personal pressures increased, Bonhoeffer could not escape the choice between exile and resistance. To choose one or the other was necessary; to choose one and yet be able to affirm both required a new sort of faith, a movement beyond the dichotomizing, identity-defining structures that served him in the Church Struggle and toward the inclusive structures that characterize a more mature faith.

The closing of the seminary at Finkenwalde and the

approach of war in Europe brought pressure on Bonhoeffer not only to invent a new style of working, but to make a radical change in his way of understanding the work. These pressures began with differences, now apparent, between Bonhoeffer and the Confessing Church leadership over the role of the church in the Nazi state. While the Confessing Church leadership struggled for a religious witness, distinct from political goals and actions, Bonhoeffer was increasingly drawn toward the implementation of his "spoke in the wheel" image from 1933.[26]

When the Confessing Church in 1938 recognized the right of the state to demand an oath of loyalty to Hitler, Bonhoeffer sensed that his own commitments had outgrown the stance of the Confessing Church, and he could no longer think and work exclusively within its structure.

With the active, effective life of the Confessing Church largely past and the prospect of a military call-up in the immediate future, Bonhoeffer now confronted in a direct and personal way the alternative of exile and resistance. While he struggled in the backwoods of Pomerania, his beloved older brother, Klaus, was in Berlin, moving deeper into an active anti-Nazi conspiracy, along with Rüdiger Schleicher and Hans von Dohnanyi, the husbands of his sisters, Ursula and Christine. Meanwhile, Sabine was preparing for exile with her husband, Gerhard Leibholz, a lawyer of Jewish ancestry. Dietrich drove them to the Swiss border on the night of September 9, 1938, and his twin sister left their homeland to seek refuge in England.

Bonhoeffer's movement toward involvement in the secular world of action was made with characteristic deliberation and hesitation. One sees again the false starts and reconsiderations by which Bonhoeffer signaled his reluctance to bind himself to a decision until the decision was truly inevitable. He had come to Finkenwalde, as he had gone to England in 1932, on a leave of absence from his previous position. Now he sought to delay the confrontation between his pacifist convictions and the military call-up by seeking an invitation to teach and study abroad.

Thus Bonhoeffer returned to New York in June of 1939. He insisted from the outset that he was not a refugee, though his American friends at first expected and then entreated him to stay with them permanently. The undoing of their plans and Bonhoeffer's hasty return to Germany in July is a story well known, as is the letter of explanation that Bonhoeffer wrote to Reinhold Niebuhr:

> I have come to the conclusion that I have made a mistake in coming to America. I must live through this difficult period of our national history with the Christian people of Germany. I will have no right to participate in the reconstruction of Christian life in Germany after the war if I do not share in the trials of this time with my people.[27]

The decision to "share in the trials of this time with my people" was crucial for Bonhoeffer; and he would refer to it again from his cell in Tegel as a source of meaning for all that he had undergone. To understand this decision within the framework of Bonhoeffer's faith, however, we cannot read it in isolation. His personal choice against exile must be considered in context with remarks on American church life that he wrote on the way back to Europe.

In Bonhoeffer's mind, the different roles of the refugee and the witness to truth were now linked with the different styles of church life in Germany and America. The historic, confessional *Landeskirchen* of Germany are witnesses to decisions about basic truths. The American churches, made up of successive waves of refugees, are organized around a different value.

In the sanctuary there is no longer a place for strife. Confessional stringency and intolerance must cease for the person who has himself shunned intolerance. . . . To abstain from the final settlement of the question of truth remains the hardest task for the Christian fugitive all his life. All that can be convincing for him in America is the deep earnestness and unbounded extent of the concern and the right of sanctuary in the land of his refuge. . . . It is in the last resort faithfulness to its own church history which is expressed in this peculiar relativism of the question of truth in the thought and action of American Christianity.[28]

The church of the refugee, then, cannot be a "confessing church"; but the refugee, nonetheless, has a valid witness. Thus, the question for Bonhoeffer in 1939 is: What is God saying to us and to the Americans through our different church experiences?

Both the Americans and ourselves are concerned with the same word, the same commandment, the same promise, and the same office and the same community of Jesus Christ. And only this question does justice to the situation.[29]

We see in this essay the paradoxical-consolidative structures of Bonhoeffer's mature faith. The Christian witness is preserved through a multiplicity of valid alternatives that are mutually exclusive, and yet mutually implicatory. This is not a religion of pure tolerance or indifference, since each Christian must still make the choice between exile and resistance, and each choice imposes its own costs. But the identity-defining choice is set in the context of other choices, which are also witnesses to truth, and which speak with insistent voices that must be heard alongside one's own.

The range of valid alternatives, of course, is not infinitely wide. The German who confuses his loyalty to Christ with his loyalty to Hitler is still wrong. What is new is the recognition that there are forms of loyalty to Christ different from his own, which indeed he could not adopt for himself, but which still could not be excluded as invalid.

This introduces into the life of any single believer an ambiguity that is not simply an *absurdum* to be disciplined out of the Christian life, but an integral part of what it means to live as a committed Christian. Because the Christian faith cannot be reduced to one single style of life or one single witness, one can never rest in simpleminded confidence that one's own life has captured all the essentials and excluded all the betrayals. Increasingly after 1939, Bonhoeffer saw engagement with this ambiguity, rather than retreat from it, as the essential feature of the Christian life.

Thus he wrote from Tegel:

For a long time . . . I thought I could acquire faith by trying to live a holy life, or something like it. I suppose I wrote *The Cost of Discipleship* as the end of that path. Today I see the dangers of that book, though I still stand by what I wrote.

I discovered later, and I'm still discovering right up to this moment, that it is only by living completely in this world that one learns to have faith. One must completely abandon any attempt to make something of oneself, whether it be saint, or a converted sinner, or a churchman (a so-called priestly type!), a righteous man or an unrighteous one, a sick man or a healthy one.[30]

The structure of faith that enabled Bonhoeffer to face the choices before him in 1939 gave shape to both his thought and his work in the years that followed. His *Ethics,* much of which was written in intervals of concentrated theological work between the demands of his wartime assignments, shows us how he progressively came to grips with the problems of Christian action in an essentially ambiguous situation. Always there is the insistence that problems must be faced in their full reality, not masked by generalities that are easily spoken but convey no specific meaning and invite no serious response. Thus the confession of guilt that he prepared for the churches in 1940 takes up in concrete terms the burden of the churches' failures that led to the horrors of Nazism:

> The Church confesses that she has witnessed in silence the spoliation and exploitation of the poor and the enrichment and corruption of the strong.
> The Church confesses herself guilty towards the countless victims of calumny, denunciation and defamation. She has not convicted the slanderer of his wrongdoing, and she has thereby abandoned the slandered to his fate.
> The Church confesses that she has desired security, peace and quiet, possessions and honour, to which she had no right, and that in this way she has not bridled the desires of men, but has stimulated them still further.[31]

At the same time, there is in the *Ethics* the recognition that concrete human actions can never be exhaustively justified by abstract moral principles or general truths about human history. Always there remains, for the one who takes the responsibility for *this* specific action, the guilt incurred for results that go beyond one's careful intentions, and the need for forgiveness.

It was in just this spirit of a "venture of responsibility"[32] that Bonhoeffer developed his own active participation in the German resistance to Hitler. This resistance was centered in the Army General Staff under General Beck and in the *Abwehr* (military intelligence) under Admiral Canaris and his deputy, Colonel Hans Oster. Hans von Dohnanyi, Dietrich's brother-in-law, was an *Abwehr* lawyer actively involved in the resistance group under Oster as early as 1938.

Dietrich, his brothers, and his brothers-in-law were thus in the confidence of the *Abwehr* conspirators from the beginning, and Dietrich became an active participant late in 1940. *Gestapo* prohibitions against publishing and public speaking had almost ended Dietrich's usefulness as a traveling "visitor" for the Confessing Church, so he accepted Hans' offer to procure him an assignment as a civilian agent for the *Abwehr*. He was registered with the Munich office, a move that protected him both from the military call-up and from the suspicious surveillance of the *Gestapo* in East Prussia and Berlin. In this capacity, Dietrich was actively involved in the plans that led eventually to the attempt on Hitler's life on July 20, 1944.

Bonhoeffer, as we have seen, spoke out as early as 1933 on the legitimacy of Christian action against a state running out of control. Unlike many in the Confessing Church, who to the end would eschew political resistance and who after the war would still refuse to honor the "political martyrdom" of Dietrich Bonhoeffer, Bonhoeffer himself could accommodate action against Hitler in the name of Christ.

What inhibited his action, it seems, was not the idea of resistance, but the ambiguity of any particular form of resistance. An effective conspiracy may, indeed, "put the spoke in the wheel," but conspiracy requires in the execution deceit, suspicion, danger to the lives of innocent friends and family, and finally murder—all without any guarantee of success. If the conspirators failed, they would be repudiated as traitors. If they succeeded, they had no assurance that their action would win any concessions from the Allies toward the German people. This Bonhoeffer knew all too well from the clandestine contacts he made with the English Bishop George Bell during the War. The peace feelers he secretly carried from the conspirators in Berlin to Bell in Stockholm were answered from London by renewed demands for unconditional surrender.

Moreover, Bonhoeffer remembered very well the contempt of the German people for the "traitors" believed responsible for Germany's humiliation at Versailles after World War I. Even a successful *coup d'etat* and a speedy conclusion to the war would not vindicate the conspirators.

With no assured justification from history or morality, Bonhoeffer could enter the conspiracy only as the outcome of his choice to share in the sufferings of the German people. Conscious always that he might have chosen otherwise, he always resisted offering easy moral sanctions for the conspiracy. This is apparent in the short paragraph headed, "No ground under our feet":

> One may ask whether there have ever before in human history been people with so little ground under their feet—people to whom every available alternative seemed equally intolerable, repugnant, and futile, who looked beyond all these existing alternatives for the source of their strength so entirely in the past or in the future, and who yet, without being dreamers, were able to await the success of their cause so quietly and confidently.[33]

Bonhoeffer's new ability to rest content and even secure in an ambiguous situation extended into his personal life during the war years. We have already noted that in the early years of the Church Struggle he had been close to a young woman in Berlin. He maintained a correspondence with her from London, but as we have seen, he devoted himself to the life of the seminary at Finkenwalde in a way that seemed to preclude any personal romance.[34]

Bonhoeffer's opinion of marriage was much altered by the fall of 1941, when he visited Switzerland on an assignment from the *Abwehr*. In Switzerland he took the opportunity to visit his old friend from Union Seminary days, Erwin Sutz. Sutz had recently married, and

Bonhoeffer afterward wrote some reflections on their visit:

> It was always clear to me that one may only take this step as a Christian in a strong faith and in view of God's mercy. For by this act one desires, in the midst of general destruction, to build; in the midst of life from hour to hour and day to day, one desires a future; in the midst of our exile from the earth, some living space; in the midst of the general misery, a bit of happiness. And the amazing thing is that to this singular desire, God says, "Yes," that here God concurs with our desire, although we would expect the opposite.[35]

Bonhoeffer was now apparently ready to claim some of this "living space" for himself. In the spring of 1942, during a visit to the estate of a friend and supporter of the Confessing Church, he encountered the eighteen-year-old Maria von Wedemeyer. The girl quickly captured the imagination and affection of the older theologian. In the following months, as the conspiracy against Hitler moved toward its climax, one of the conspirators was also involved in a deeply personal project. On January 17, 1943, Dietrich Bonhoeffer and Maria von Wedemeyer were quietly engaged.

The year 1943, then, might have marked a turning point in Bonhoeffer's personal life and in his career, but the promise of the engagement and his hopes for the conspiracy were interrupted by a series of arrests on April 5, in which Bonhoeffer, his sister Christine, and her husband, Hans von Dohnanyi, were all imprisoned. Although Bonhoeffer never gave up hope for his release, and often wrote letters about his plans for marriage and theological work after the war, his poetry suggests that he sensed the truth of the matter; this was the end of his active career. The next "station" on the road to freedom would be suffering:

A change has come indeed. Your hands, so strong and active,
are bound; in helplessness now you see your action
is ended; you sigh in relief, your cause committing
to stronger hands; so now you may rest contented.
Only for one blissful moment would you draw near to touch
    freedom;
then, that it might be perfected in glory, you gave it to God.[36]

Amazingly, however, the authorities were still unaware of the full extent of the *Abwehr* conspiracy, and Bonhoeffer and his associates were held on rather unimportant charges at first. Bonhoeffer was taken to the military prison at Tegel, a suburb of Berlin.

Once he had adjusted to this confinement, Bonhoeffer seized the opportunity to reflect on the path his faith had taken since 1939 and on what this new direction might mean for the future of his church. We have noted already some of his written reflections during this period, and especially his remarks on the transition in his own faith from the search for a secure identity to an acceptance of life in its ambiguity. *Letters and Papers from Prison* is a rich source of such reflections on the past, but beginning with a letter to Eberhard Bethge on April 30, 1944, Bonhoeffer's thoughts take a new theological turn, toward the life of the Christian in the present: "What is bothering me incessantly is the question what Christianity really is, or indeed who Christ really is, for us today?"[37]

What emerges in these last fragments from the prison years, then, is Bonhoeffer's attempt to solve for the church the problem he had faced for himself in 1939, the problem of religious identity in a world of ambiguity. In the company of those of different faiths and of no faith, he had undertaken the risky business of restoring a world in which human life could be lived freely and responsibly. This task had taken him outside the accepted boundaries of Christian action, but he wasted no time in prison on self-justification or recrimination. His task was rather to show how the church could embrace the ambiguities of life in the modern world as he had, and so find its life not in the purity of its proclamation, but in service.

> The church is the church only when it exists for others. To make a start, it should give away all its property to those in need. The clergy must live solely on the free-will offerings of their congregations, or possibly engage in some secular calling. The church must share in the secular problems of ordinary human life, not dominating, but helping and serving. It must tell men of every calling what it means to live in Christ, to exist for others.[38]

In this late fragment of theology, the conclusion to a brief outline for a book, we see Bonhoeffer's transition from an individuating faith to a consolidating faith carried to its conclusion and applied to the life of the church. The task of the church is now no longer chiefly to establish itself by asserting the uniqueness of its confession or by demanding recognition of its privileged position in society. The church can be itself only by giving itself away, by surrendering itself to the needs of the world around it. For the church, as for Bonhoeffer himself, identity is no longer something to be achieved; it is the outcome of engagement with reality as it confronts us. The servant of Jesus Christ in the church must be the servant of the world.

How far Bonhoeffer was able to carry these new thoughts in his own mind we shall probably never know. On July 20, 1944, an attempt on Hitler's life failed, and by autumn the *Gestapo* had fully uncovered the conspiracy. Dietrich was transferred to a maximum security prison and isolated from his family and friends. He carried with him only a few books and, probably, a packet of notes with which he had begun to fill out the outline for his new work.

His life was now caught up in the race between

Germany's impending military collapse and Hitler's insatiable vengeance. In the spring of 1945, prisoners were shunted from prison to prison to avoid the increasingly heavy allied attacks, and any particular prisoner wanted for a particular purpose might sometimes remain unlocated in the general confusion. Bonhoeffer was finally traced by two special agents of the Reich Security Head Office to a temporary prison in Schoenberg, a small hamlet in Bavaria. In spite of the military situation, a vehicle was requisitioned and fuel was found to take the prisoner Bonhoeffer to the concentration camp at Flossenbürg. There, during the night of April 8-9, he was confronted with the other members of the conspiracy for the last time and sentenced to death by a military tribunal. Early on the morning of April 9, the prisoners were hanged in the woods outside the camp.

Some Questions That Remain

Bonhoeffer never fully articulated his vision of the world come of age, and he never completed his sketch of the church for that world. There are indications, however, that his own faith underwent a further transformation, that he moved beyond the acquiescence of the obedient servant to a heartfelt, even joyful, acceptance of the role he had been called to play. This new faith never becomes fully explicit; it appears primarily in the prison poetry and is confirmed chiefly by the reports of those who in various ways shared the last months of captivity with him.

In a poem written after more than a year in prison, Bonhoeffer asked, "Who am I?" and contrasted his internal longings and anxieties with the reports of others that he "would step from my cell's confinement calmly, cheerfully, firmly, like a squire from his country-house." The poem continues:

DIETRICH BONHOEFFER

Who am I? They often tell me
I would talk to my warders
freely and friendly and clearly,
as though it were mine to command.

Who am I? They also tell me
I would bear the days of misfortune
equably, smilingly, proudly,
like one accustomed to win.[39]

Harold Poelchau, the chaplain at Tegel while Bonhoeffer was there, reports that toward his fellow prisoners
and warders he was exactly as his poem describes him.
Dietrich became a pastor to fellow prisoners and guards
alike, and others who were in prison with him remember
him as a source of hope and comfort.[40]
The prison fragments are replete with passages that
testify to his love for life; yet he could also write:

Come now, thou greatest of feasts on the
   journey to freedom eternal;
death, cast aside all the burdensome chains,
   and demolish the walls of our temporal body,
   the walls of our souls that are blinded,
so that at last we may see that which here remains hidden.
Freedom, how long we have sought thee in discipline,
   action, and suffering;
dying, we now may behold thee revealed in the Lord.[41]

Fowler maintains that there is a crucifixion involved in
seeing and accepting the inevitabilities of certain tragic
denouements in history. Bonhoeffer's love of life, balanced against his sense that its meaning is hidden in death,
is surely an example of some of the agony that
accompanies this final stage of faith development.
   Toward the end of his time in Tegel, Bonhoeffer was

fascinated with the figure of Moses, the "man of God and prophet" who died as he looked over the promised land of his people. From that perspective, Moses could see that all his experience and all the experiences of his people could be understood in relationship to the fidelity of God:

> So you fulfill, Lord, that which you promise.
> Never have you broken your word to me.
>
> Whether words of favor or of judgment,
> Always they came to pass.

What Moses sees from the mountaintop, however, is not the past. It is a vision of the kingdom, the promised land into which his people will enter.

> God's land! Before your wide gate we stand
> Blessed, lost as in a dream.
>
> Already the benedictions of the Patriarchs
> Blow upon us, full of power and of promise.
>
> God's vineyard, fresh bedecked with dew,
> Heavy clusters, sparkling in the sunshine.
>
> God's garden, swelling with your fruits,
> Clear water springing from your wells.
>
> God's grace over free earth,
> Where a new and holy people shall come to be.
>
> God's justice between strong and weak
> Will stand guard over decree and power.

For twenty-eight stanzas, Bonhoeffer, always so careful to focus proper attention on the present, concrete reality, nevertheless allows himself here to revel in the eschatological vision, which comes to a climax in Moses' exclamation:

Wake up, take hold! It is not a dream.
God has done well by weary hearts.
Behold the splendor of the promised land;
All is yours, and you are set free!

But freedom for Moses is not the liberty to take possession. His is a liberation of a different order:

Sinking, O God, into your eternities,
I see my people enter into freedom.
You who punish sin and gladly forgive,
God, I have loved this people.
That I carried their disgrace and their burdens,
And I have seen their salvation—that is enough.
Keep me! Hold me! My staff has fallen.
Faithful God, prepare for me my grave.[42]

Was this, the faith of Moses, also the final form of Bonhoeffer's faith? Was the universalizing vision in which all things are related to God and God's kingdom becomes a present, tangible reality a real part of Bonhoeffer's experience in the closing months of his life? The evidence is inconclusive, but it does suggest that in his imprisonment, he was moving in that direction. Had Bonhoeffer truly reached the point where death could be received as the final station on the road to freedom, or was his poem a reach for a stage that he longed for but had not yet attained?

These questions cannot be answered with finality, but what can be said certainly is chiseled beneath his memorial in the Flossenbürg Church: "Dietrich Bonhoeffer—a witness to Jesus Christ among his brethren."[43]

Bibliography

For English readers, the definitive biography of Bonhoeffer is available in translation:
Bethge, Eberhard. *Dietrich Bonhoeffer: Man of Vision, Man of Courage.* New York: Harper & Row, 1970.

An excellent short biography is:

Bosanquet, Mary. *The Life and Death of Dietrich Bonhoeffer.* New York: Harper & Row, 1969.

Some of Bonhoeffer's works are available in English translation, including:

The Cost of Discipleship. 2nd ed. New York:Macmillan, 1959.

Ethics. New York: Macmillan, 1965.

Letters and Papers from Prison. New York: Macmillan, 1972.

A comprehensive biography of Bonhoeffer materials in English is available in:

Green, Clifford J. "Bonhoeffer Bibliography: English Language Sources," *Union Seminary Quarterly Review,* Summer 1976, 227-60.

Selections from the German *Gesammelte Schriften* have been translated and arranged chronologically under the editorship of E. H. Robertson and published by Harper & Row, 1965-73:

No Rusty Swords: Letters, Lectures, and Notes, 1928–36.

The Way to Freedom: Letters, Lectures, and Notes, 1935–39.

True Patriotism: Letters, Lectures, and Notes, 1939–45.

Conclusion

We have traced five trajectories in faith, told the stories of five lives with the aid of a stage theory of faith development. Now we want to consider what we have learned about these subjects as a group—and about ourselves—from the investigations.

It is apparent that generalization about these five subjects will be the hardest task. What impresses us most about them is the uniqueness of each, and the stage theory does not provide any simple objective standards by which their personal qualities can be reduced to a common formula. The sequence of developmental stages is a tool for the biographer; it helps us to identify the turning points in individual lives and provides clues for interpreting the dramatic personal transformations that often characterize great leaders and great intellects.

In the first instance a faith development biography is useful because it gives coherence to the individual life that is under study. When faith is conceived as a comprehensive way of construing the world, we can sometimes see a fundamental faith orientation that emerges very early in life and endures even through radical changes in a person's stated "beliefs." Bonhoeffer's attempt to grasp an ambiguous world as an aesthetic whole appeared in his musical aptitude and interests before he became a theologian. Wittgenstein wrestled with language and its limits in his engineering problems and in his studies in mechanics long before he found the philosophical system that allowed him to address the problem directly. Indeed, in some cases a faith orientation may never come to full articulation, because no adequate way is found to express a new comprehension of reality that is at odds with a prevailing ideology. The case of Anne Hutchinson in the Massachusetts Bay Colony appears to be an example of this.

Much as we may learn about individual lives, these studies leave us with the urge to generalize. Faith development theory may illuminate the faith of Anne Hutchinson or Ludwig Wittgenstein or Dietrich Bonhoeffer, but does their faith tell us anything about faith in general? Does it tell us anything about our own faith?

We think that it does. Probing the consciousness of persons who have lived on the outer limits of faith always has a curious reflexive quality. A faith development biography is not only an investigation of the subject; it is at the same time an exploration of the investigator and the investigative model. Faith development theory may tell us much about Malcolm X, but, as James Fowler notes, Malcolm in his turn tells us some things about the theory and its limits, and about who we are ourselves.

As a preliminary summary of these studies we offer the following conclusions:

1) Faith is a continuous personal process. Seen in a developmental perspective, even radical transformations can be understood as parts of a coherent whole. The underlying unity of faith that we find in Bonhoeffer or Wittgenstein probably characterizes all human life and provides a continuity of intention and concern that is more durable than most other elements in personal identity. Faith is a source of integrity, not only because it gives wholeness to our world at any given time, but because it provides continuity in our lives through time.

2) Within this process of faith, if allowed to run its course, there will inevitably be times when faith is neither comfortable to the one who lives it nor congenial to others close at hand. Continuing growth in faith requires a movement beyond conventional social adjustment to the style of individuative-reflective faith, which often construes the world in terms of powerful oppositions. Those who live fully in this stage will become the disturbing nonconformists, the zealous disciples, or the demanding leaders. The developmental process requires, moreover, that these tensions and dichotomies eventually become disturbing even for the one who draws them, for that is the dynamic by which faith moves on to a new stage that makes possible a genuine acceptance of the paradoxes of human existence.

3) Faith is a way of giving coherence to our world. To know the world comprehensively is to be totally engaged with it, volitionally and affectively, as well as cognitively. The relationships that bind us to other persons and to shared centers of meaning and value obviously cannot be reduced to our ideas about them, and the faith that holds these relationships in a complex unity must encompass our loving, as well as our thinking. A careful examination of faith, especially at its highest stages, leads us to reconceive knowledge as active, personal involvement. This is not a new idea, of course. It is as old as Plato's *Symposium*. But the force of the idea is often lost in an age that models knowledge on detached, scientific observation. A study of Bonhoeffer or Pascal invites us to recover an older understanding.

Let us consider these summary conclusions in more detail:

Perhaps the most insistent claim of faith-development theory is that faith is a continuous process. The transitions and transformations in a person's faith are not just random series of opinions charted through time. Rather, each stage of faith proceeds from the one before it and continues a basic project of faith that is a lifetime occupation. The continuity of faith, then, is not the persistence of a finished set of beliefs. It is the continual testing and reformulation that keeps beliefs alive precisely by ensuring that they do *not* become reduced to fixed ideas.

This assertion of continuity is at first a bit puzzling when it is applied to Wittgenstein, whose philosophical work falls into two distinct periods, or to Malcolm X, whose abrupt and seemingly unpredictable conversions marked radical transformations in his personal attachments and values. Nevertheless, the developmental theory can accommodate these changes within the framework of its stages, and can suggest the dynamics that lead from one position to another, even when the two phases of a subject's life seem to be sharply opposed.

Any biographical study tends to moderate these contrasts by filling in the details of private experience that link public speeches or writings from very different and sometimes distant periods. The developmental approach to faith biography carries this approach one step further by focusing our attention on the structural characteristics of faith at each point in a person's life. When this is done, the sequence of orientations, in spite of changes that occur, appears as a coherent whole. Each new formulation emerges as a response to the distinctive problems posed by the previous stage, and the sequence as a whole forms a continuous "trajectory." Discrete and even apparently contradictory commitments, when organized structurally according to a developmental schema, may reveal themselves as different engagements of a persistent set of issues posed with increasing complexity and self-awareness at each new stage of development.

Thus, in spite of the vast differences in content that separate Wittgenstein's *Tractatus* from his *Philosophical Investigations,* Linell Cady's study suggests a link between them in the structural transition from a dichotomizing to a consolidative way of dealing with the fundamental problems that his experience posed. The struggle with the trivial and delusive styles of culture in late Habsburg Vienna marked Wittgenstein's thinking for life, and his development as a philosopher reflects the transformation of a faith that seeks to comprehend a world that is often hidden from us by the very language we use to describe it.

The focus on structural changes in faith does not minimize questions of content. The philosophical questions posed in the early work of Wittgenstein are no less important because we can trace their transformation into other, different questions in the mind of the man who raised them. The world-embracing explorations of Dietrich Bonhoeffer are structurally similar to the explorations of his older contemporary, Martin Heidegger, but Bonhoeffer became a hero of the German resistance, while Heidegger, at least for a time, was counted among the Nazis.[1] Such examples should dispel the notion that a structural approach to faith provides automatic answers to hard questions of philosophy and morality.

A structural approach to faith development does, however, provide us with a way of understanding human integrity by relating what we often see as discrete and contradictory systems of ideas to a more basic personal endeavor. Faith is the attempt to organize complex and conflicting experiences into a universe, a whole and coherent reality. In the dynamics of development a person must find some way to test the structures of faith against the challenges of unfolding experience. In Bonhoeffer the challenge was to conform his own life and the life of his church to a Christ who required radical obedience and whose leadership could not be shared, either with the *Fuehrer*, who demanded unquestioning loyalty, or with the self-centered demands of his own personality. Wittgenstein, too, imposed uncompromising standards. The search for meaning could not be limited; it determined his friendships and his life-style as well as his philosophy. Pascal and Anne Hutchinson, contemporaries in spite of all the differences between them, determined to give coherence to their lives out of a personal experience of meaning at a time when conventional systems of faith could resist them with all the sanctions of political and moral authority. Malcolm X inspired his people with a hope for liberation that was not a platform for racial politics, but a complete account of personal and social life that offered dignity and security in an environment that threatened destruction. The trajectories we have examined show us the integrity of a faith that is tested, a faith that may undergo radical revisions, but that takes on the awesome task of making sense of the whole world, all at once.

Faith development, if unobstructed and ongoing, entails a movement beyond the conventional truths of society into a more rigorous, autonomous search for one's own truth. The trajectories that we trace in these studies are not straightforward transitions from conventional wisdom to magnanimous personal visions that take the whole world within their sweep. The change comes, rather, through an individuating faith in which a preliminary truth is passionately held and aggressively extended into all areas of life. Subtle distinctions are absorbed into polar contrasts, and some new valence—good or bad, friend or foe—must be attached to everything that comes into view. This faith, the individuative-reflective faith, is one of the most puzzling and intriguing phenomena we encounter in the study of faith development biographies. It is the faith of Bonhoeffer during the Church Struggle and of Malcolm X during his most intense commitment to black exclusivism. It is the faith of Pascal in the intense and sometimes bitter humor of the *Provincial Letters,* or the faith of Wittgenstein during his estrangement from

Russell. It is a faith that inspires the devoted allegiance of the seminarians at Finkenwelde to their director, but that may also elicit the strident rejection that cast Anne Hutchinson from Massachusetts Bay as "being a woman not fit for our society."

It is easy to criticize an individuative-reflective faith. To the more conventional believers, it appears as a violation of common sense, to be condemned not so much because it is untrue as because it is excessive. If individuative faith sometimes inspires rage, it also elicits indulgent humor, especially from those whose own development has passed this stage of the need for sharp dichotomies or who may have removed themselves intellectually to a comfortable ironic distance from their society's conflicts. An older scholar's characterization of Bonhoeffer as "a highly-gifted but now altogether fanatical teacher" is typical of this response.[2]

Stage 4 faith is thus subject to rejection from above and below. It stands those who live within it on rather narrow ground, and we should not be surprised to find that no one takes it up lightly. While many adolescents and young adults will attempt a stage 4 stance in an all-absorbing response to a charismatic figure, the leaders who themselves inspire this devotion and who formulate the positions that draw sharp lines for great historic conflicts are necessarily rather rare. It is at this point, more than at any other, that the structural-developmental study of faith biography seems to bear out Erik Erikson's thesis that greatness arises when the conflicts within society happen to mirror the tensions between a restless, brilliant individual and his or her own environment. In such cases, it seems, the social controversy has a capacity to release personal energies that would otherwise be dissipated in unresolved tension, or perhaps, in a more solidly conventional environment, might never be aroused. It is not surprising, then, that many of the figures we have studied rose to prominence against a background of social change that particularly affected their families and their social class. Bonhoeffer and Wittgenstein were the products of an *haut-bourgeosie* that was propelled to social dominance by the decline of the imperial aristocracies of Germany and Austria. Malcolm X matured in the Northern urban environment that was a new home for many American blacks. Anne Hutchinson aroused vehement opposition because her charismatic leadership threatened the still uncertain sources of authority in a community that had just established a whole new set of social boundaries amidst the intimacies, hardships, and uncertainties of the first colonial settlements.

An individuative-reflective faith is a drive toward answers that do not yet exist, and it is inevitable that this drive will upset those who prefer to stay with what they know until a substantial replacement has been formulated, tested, and pronounced satisfactory. In the end, however, an individuating faith not only discomfits the conventional observer; its polar tensions become unbearable for the subject. In stage 4, faith is curiously divided against itself. The drive toward a unity of meaning and value breaks down the conventional frame of reference and selects a few overarching values under which all experience is to be subsumed. The stark contrasts between these basic values, however, tend to polarize experience rather than to unify it. We are uncomfortable with the figures who live most intensely in this stage not only because they seem susceptible to a fanatical narrowness, but because they seem sometimes to be denying the ultimate unity that faith is seeking in experience. Their faith is almost dualistic, rather than unifying, and unless they are overwhelmed by their own commitments to the struggle they have chosen, these men and women of profound faith are ultimately driven by their own internal striving to seek answers beyond the terms of the conflicts they have precipitated.

The final irony of the world transformer, then, is that this man or woman often moves beyond followers and adversaries who have accepted the terms of the stage 4 polarities. Bonhoeffer gradually shifted his center of activity away from the Confessing Church. Exiled to Rhode Island, Anne Hutchinson simply refused to hear the representatives of Massachusetts Bay, who were themselves still obsessed with their inability to resolve the conflict she had provoked. Upon Malcolm's return from the pilgrimages to Mecca, his followers in Harlem saw his commitment to a widened understanding of humanity as a sellout and a betrayal.

When the sharp lines of division have been blurred by experience, and the instinct for self-vindication has been tempered by real victories and real defeats, then faith can proceed with the task of unification that it intended in the beginning; but there is no straight path from the exploration of a world of conventional possibilities to a *univ*erse that has personal meaning for oneself. That goal is reached only by a path of passionate commitment, even if to a partial truth, and the unity that is finally achieved will always have the character of a reconciliation, not simply an intellectual synthesis.

It is this quality of reconciliation that makes the highest levels of faith development so elusive. When we write about faith in academic terms, we are apt to judge its adequacy by its resolution of the perennial human problems: suffering, injustice, tragedy, and death. Conceptual adequacy is an important dimension of evaluation, but it is not the only measure of progress in faith development.

Because faith is, as we said at the outset, a continuous *personal* process, we must acknowledge the personal, affective dimension in all faith-knowing. Our interest in the world is from the beginning bound up with our loving and needing. Without the motivation that begins with the infant's restless desire for mutuality with the world mediated by the mother, we would not explore the world at all. And where this motivation is weak or absent, the complex structuring of experiences and expectations that we call faith simply does not get started.

That early relationship between affection and cognition is generally acknowledged by psychologists, but the studies in this volume suggest that the observation is equally valid in later stages of faith development. The identity-defining dichotomies of stage 4 faith are never established with the cool objectivity of a botanist classifying field grasses. They are commitments that engage our capacities for love and hate, and they touch the instinctual sources of emotional energy so directly that those who live in this stage 4 faith often seem to pursue their visions with almost super-human persistence and determination.

The concept of God, no less than the structuring of reality, is shaped by this affective intensity. God, the sometimes familiar, sometimes mysterious presence understood by synthetic-conventional faith, suddenly overwhelms all the categories by which stage 3 integrates the ultimate and incomprehensible into the workaday world. God becomes the judge, demanding a decision at every moment about every sphere of life, drawing one part of the world into total loyalty to himself and casting another into permanent opposition. In this sense our observation that there is no easy path from the interpersonal familiarity of stage 3 to the paradoxical acceptance of opposites in stage 5, parallels Whitehead's remark that in religion the step between God the Void and God the Companion is God the Enemy.[3] The God of individuative-reflective faith may not be *our* enemy. Often, he is our enemy's enemy. But always his reality is perceived through our strongest powers of love and hate.

This accounts for the quality of reconciliation at the highest stages of faith development. They come at the end of a personal journey when it becomes possible to imagine that God loves what I hate, when there is some glimmer of sense to the suggestion that God loves even what *he* hates.

At this point in faith development, it is not enough to say that the world recovers a formal, structural unity. It is more complete and accurate to say, with Paul, that "God is reconciling the world to himself." Conceptual formulations of this reconciliation are possible. Indeed, for most of the figures in this volume, they are central. Bonhoeffer and Pascal exemplify this abstract, verbal, and rational mode of understanding within the traditional religious framework, as Wittgenstein does outside of it. These biographical studies should, however, make us wary of separating the conceptual achievement too neatly from the affective movement that accompanies and sustains it. In faith, the conceptual synthesis of the world is integrated with a volitional commitment to the world, and it is only when these two movements become one that we have genuine knowledge. Faith achieves a loving affirmation of reality as a whole that Jonathan Edwards and the New England Theology called "consent."

This is a term whose meaning we have largely lost. Consent has become something we give reluctantly to a surgical procedure of last resort, something voted by a surly Senate in response to a diplomatic *fait accompli*. In its original meaning, however, consent is a true and total union of will with reality, an ecstatic movement, really. In consent the tension between what we know is the case and what we believe ought to be is surpassed, rather than suppressed. It is a movement in which our duty and our delight become one.

This is the most difficult structure of relationships, in which the self becomes a part of the totality with which faith wrestles, and the subject becomes available to others with nothing reserved, nothing held back or hidden. This is the end point of the trajectories we have studied, the stage that our subjects either finally achieved or at last came near enough to, to struggle for.

We see it best, perhaps, where love is joined to withdrawal, and resignation is fused with hope: Bonhoeffer's simple leave-taking from his fellow prisoners on an April Sunday in the little village of Schoenberg; Anne Hutchinson, a "deare saint," dearer to her followers than the church, widow and exile, closing her life in isolation on a rural farmstead; Ludwig Wittgenstein, lonely and self-tormented, sending the final message, "Tell them I've had a wonderful life."

If it is difficult to specify conceptually the structure of this universalizing faith, it is perhaps harder still to define with precision the characteristics that distinguish it from its nearest imitations, to distinguish a high quality of thinking *about* the world from a faithful engagement *with* the world.

Nevertheless, the difference is real in experience. There are those lives in whom the relationship to the ultimate environment is more than a solution to their own search for selfhood. It becomes a way of giving themselves to and for others. Such persons are ready for fellowship with persons at any of the other stages and from any other faith tradition. They seem to know instinctively how to relate to us affirmingly, never condescendingly, yet with pricks to our pretentiousness and with gifts of the genuine bread of life.

There is a tradition in theology that holds that we can truly love another individual only when that particular other is loved in the context of a loving affirmation of reality as a whole. Our modern emphasis on the quality of individual interpersonal relationships makes us skeptical of such generalized love, but our encounters with those who live a universalizing faith can convince us again of that love's reality and power. Limited as we are by the narrowness of our own horizons, it is easier to say where we have experienced this than to specify what we have experienced. Questions about the limits of faith are better asked by *who* than by *how*. And that, perhaps, is the best justification for the studies we have undertaken in this volume.

Notes

Introduction

1. *La Legende Doree*, ed. Teodor de Wyzewa (Paris: Librairie Academique, 1929), p. 580.
2. *Two Early Tudor Lives*, ed. Richard S. Sylvester and Davis P. Harding (New Haven: Yale University Press, 1962), p. 238.
3. From the Latin preface to the English *Book of Martyrs* of 1563. Quoted in J. F. Mozley, *John Foxe and His Book* (London: SPCK, 1940), pp. 133-34.
4. See, for example, Mary Bushnell Cheney, *The Life and Letters of Horace Bushnell* (New York, 1880); William C. Gannet, *Ezra Stiles Gannet* (Boston, 1875); John Weiss, *Life and Correspondence of Theodore Parker* (New York, 1864).
5. "Leonardo Da Vinci and a Memory of his Childhood." See the *Standard Edition* of Freud's Works, vol. 11.
6. *American Journal of Psychology*, 1913, p. 360.
7. Erikson, *Young Man Luther* (New York: W. W. Norton, 1962); *Gandhi's Truth* (W. W. Norton, 1969).
8. See Erik Erikson, *Childhood and Society* (New York: W. W. Norton, 1950), pp. 247-74.
9. *Young Man Luther*, p. 22.
10. Julian Hartt, "Encounter and Inference in our Awareness of God," in *The God Experience*, ed. Joseph Whelan (New York: Newman Press, 1971), p. 49.
11. See, for example, Jean Piaget, *The Psychology of Intelligence* (New York: Littlefield, Adams & Co., 1966), chap. 5.
12. Lawrence Kohlberg, "Stage and Sequence: The Cognitive Developmental Approach to Socialization," in *Handbook of Socialization Theory and Research*, ed. David Goslin (Chicago: Rand McNally, 1969), pp. 347-480.
13. James W. Fowler, "Life/Faith Patterns: Structures of Trust and Loyalty," in Fowler and Keen, *Life Maps: Conversations on the Journey of Faith* (Waco, Tex.: Word Books, 1978), pp. 14-101; also Fowler,

"Faith and the Structuring of Meaning," paper delivered at the American Psychological Association, August 26, 1977.
14. Hartt, "Encounter and Inference," pp. 49, 52.
15. See James W. Fowler, "Stages in Faith: The Structural Developmental Perspective," in *Studies in Moral Development,* ed. Thomas Hennessey (New York: Paulist Press, 1976); and Fowler, "Faith Development Theory and the Aims of Religious Socialization," in *Emerging Issues in Religious Education,* ed. Gloria Durka and Joan-Marie Smith (Paulist Press, 1976).
16. The age range indicated for each of the stages represents a minimal age span for the initiation and consolidation of the stage. Many persons enter the stages, particularly the higher stages, at a later age than those indicated, if at all.
17. Dietrich Bonhoeffer, *No Rusty Swords,* ed. E. H. Robertson (New York: Harper & Row, 1965), pp. 92-118.
18. Ludwig Wittgenstein, *Letters to Russell, Keynes, and Moore* (Ithaca: Cornell University Press, 1974), p. 54.

1. The Pilgrimage in Faith of Malcolm X

1. Erik H. Erikson, "The Development of Ritualization," in Donald R. Cutler, ed. *The Religious Situation, 1968* (Boston: Beacon Press, 1968), pp. 711-33.
2. Malcolm X, *The Autobiography of Malcolm X* (New York: Grove Press, 1966). Quotations reprinted by permission of Random House, Inc.
3. *Autobiography,* p. 3.
4. *Ibid.,* p. 5.
5. *Ibid.,* p. 6.
6. *Ibid.,* pp. 6-7.
7. *Ibid.,* p. 8.
8. Eugene Bianchi, *The Religious Experience of Revolutionaries* (Garden City, N.Y.: Doubleday, 1972), pp. 83-108.
9. *Autobiography,* p. 14.
10. Bianchi, *The Religious Experience of Revolutionaries,* pp. 83-84.
11. Erik H. Erikson, "Autobiographic Notes on the Identity Crisis," in *Daedalus,* vol. 99, no. 4 (1970), pp. 730-59.
12. *Autobiography,* p. 36.
13. *Ibid.,* p. 48.
14. Bianchi, *The Religious Experience of Revolutionaries,* p. 85.
15. W. E. B. DuBois, *The Souls of Black Folk* (Greenwich, Conn.: Fawcett Publications, 1961), pp. 148-51.
16. *Autobiography,* pp. 169-70.
17. *Ibid.,* p. 170
18. Bianchi, *The Religious Experience of Revolutionaries,* p. 104.
19. Readers who wish to do so are urged to read Peter Goldman's excellent biography, *The Death and Life of Malcolm X* (New York: Harper & Row, 1974).

20. *Ibid.*, p. 148.
21. *Ibid.*, p. 176.
22. *Ibid.*, p. 176-77.
23. *Autobiography*, p. 306.

2. Vision and Boundaries: The Faith of Anne Hutchinson

1. R. P. Bolton, *A Woman Misunderstood* (New York: The Westchester County Historical Society, 1931), p. 4.
2. *Ibid.*, p. 7-8.
3. *Ibid.*, p. 8.
4. Note Barbara Ehrenreich and Diedre English, *Witches, Midwives, and Nurses, A History of Women Healers* (Old Westbury, N.Y.: The Feminist Press, 1973) for a fuller treatment of the relationship between women and healing.
5. David Hall, ed., *The Antinomian Controversy* (Middletown, Conn.: Wesleyan University Press, 1968), p. 226. This is a useful collection of documents from the period.
6. Winnifred Rugg, *Unafraid: A Life of Anne Hutchinson* (Boston: Beacon Press, 1930; reprinted by Books for Libraries Press, Freeport, N.Y., 1970), p. 24.
7. Hall, *The Antinomian Controversy*, p. 272.
8. *Ibid.*, p. 339.
9. *Ibid.*, p. 411 f.
10. *Ibid.*, p. 314.
11. Emory Battis, *Saints and Sectaries* (Chapel Hill: University of North Carolina Press, 1962), p. 90.
12. *Ibid.*, p. 102.
13. Hall, p. 17. "By this term she meant that the ministers were letting people 'thinke [themselves] to be saved, because they see some worke of Sanctification in them.' " More broadly, the term she used referred to the Covenant God had made with Adam. As a man without sin, Adam could ensure his salvation by fulfilling the condition of perfect obedience, but after the Fall man's "works" no longer earned him any merit with God. In the new "covenant of grace" that God established with Abraham, the sole reasons for salvation were the gospel of Christ and the free gift of grace.
14. Bolton, *A Woman Misunderstood*, p. 33.
15. Hall, *The Antinomian Controversy*, p. 17.
16. John Winthrop, *A Short Story of the Rise, Reign, and Ruine of the Antinomians, Familists & Libertines* in Hall, p. 17.
17. I. M. Lewis, *Ecstatic Religion* (Middlesex, England: Penguin Books, 1971), p. 88.
18. Kai T. Erikson, *Wayward Puritans* (New York: John Wiley & Sons, 1966), p. 67.
19. Lyle Koehler, "The Case of the American Jezebels: Anne Hutchinson

and Female Agitation during the Years of the Antinomian Turmoil 1636–1640," in *The William and Mary Quarterly*, January 1974.
20. *Ibid.*, p. 58.
21. Hall, *The Antinomian Controversy*, p. 333.
22. *Ibid.*
23. *Ibid.*, p. 434.
24. *Wayward Puritans*, p. 74.
25. *Ibid.*
26. J. MacBride Sterrett, "Antinomianism," in James Hastings, ed., *Encyclopedia of Religion and Ethics* (New York: Scribners, 1908), I, 581-82.
27. *The Antinomian Controversy*, p. 314.
28. *Ibid.*, p. 315.
29. *Ibid.*, p. 316.
30. *Ibid.*, p. 332.
31. *Ibid.*, p. 337.
32. *Ibid.*, p. 338.
33. *Ibid.*, p. 342.
34. *Ibid.*, p. 348.
35. *Ibid.*
36. Lewis, *Ecstatic Religion*, p. 89.
37. Hall, *The Antinomian Controversy*, p. 368.
38. *Ibid.*, p. 370.
39. *Ibid.*, p. 388.
40. *Ibid.*, p. 314.
11. Rugg, *Unafraid*, p. 229.
42. *Ibid.*, p. 229.
43. Bolton, *A Woman Misunderstood*, p. 92.
44. Roger Williams, quoted in Bolton, p. 103.
45. *Ibid.*

3. Toward Fire and Light: The Faith of Blaise Pascal

1. See Erik Erikson, *"The Development of Ritualization,"* in Donald R. Cutler ed., *The Religious Situation*, 1968 (Boston: Beacon Press, 1968).
2. See William F. Lynch, *Images of Hope*, (London: University of Notre Dame Press, 1966), ch. 1.
3. Steinmann describes Jacqueline Pascal at the age of eleven as being as "wholly enthusiastic about Corneille as her brother was about Euclid." She began writing her own poetry at the age of twelve. Several years later she entered and won a poetry contest which Corneille had won early in his own career. Earlier, Jacqueline had tried to win the queen's favor with her poetry in the hope that she would aid her father, Etienne.
4. Jean Steinmann, *Pascal* (London: Burns & Oates, 1965), pp. 31-32.
5. Roger Soltau, *Pascal: The Man and His Message* (West Point, Conn.; Greenwood Press, 1970), p. 47.
6. *Ibid.*, p. 53.

NOTES

7. Steinmann, *Pascal,* p. 65.
8. T. S. Eliot in the introduction to Pascal's *Pensees* (New York: E. P. Dutton, 1958), p. xiv.
9. Soltau, *Pascal: The Man and His Message,* p. 65.
10. Steinmann, *Pascal,* p. 76.
11. Blaise Pascal, in *Pascal,* vol. 33 of *Great Books of the Western World* (Chicago: Encyclopedia Britannica, 1952), *The Provincial Letters, letter 1.*
12. *Ibid.*
13. *Ibid.,* letter 5.
14. *Ibid.,* letter 17.
15. Roger Hazelton, *Blaise Pascal, The Genius of His Thought* (Philadelphia: Westminster Press, 1974), p. 19.
16. Pascal, *Pensees* (New York: E. P. Dutton, 1958), fragment 72.
17. *Ibid.*
18. *Ibid.,* fragment 465.
19. Lucien Goldmann, *The Hidden God* (London: Routledge and Kegan Paul, 1970), p. 212.
20. Jacqueline died shortly after refusing to sign the condemnation. She had been visited by a local church official who questioned her about her actions as well as about her faith. Her death is believed to have been hastened by the confrontation between the church hierarchy and the community of Port Royal.
21. See Charles S. Mackenzie, *Pascal's Anguish and Joy* (New York: Philosophical Library, 1973) p. 179.
22. Steinmann, *Pascal,* p. 191.

4. The Philosophical Passion of Ludwig Wittgenstein

1. Allan Janik and Stephen Toulmin, *Wittgenstein's Vienna* (New York: Simon & Schuster, 1973), p. 9. I have relied largely upon this work for information on the cultural situation of the Habsburg society. I highly recommend this fascinating book to anyone interested in pursuing the relation between Wittgenstein and the Viennese culture.
2. William Warren Bartley, III, *Wittgenstein* (New York: J. P. Lippincott Co., 1973). Bartley's is the only secondary work in Wittgenstein which mentions his homosexual activities.
3. Ludwig Wittgenstein, *Lectures and Conversations* (Berkeley: University of California Press, 1972), p. 59.
4. Janik and Toulmin, *Wittgenstein's Vienna,* p. 161.
5. Ludwig Wittgenstein, *Letters to Russell, Keynes and Moore* (Ithaca, N.Y.: Cornell University Press 1974), p. 16.
6. *Ibid.,* p. 45.
7. K. T. Fann, *Ludwig Wittgenstein: The Man and His Philosophy* (New York: Dell Publishing Co., 1967), p. 31.
8. *Ibid.,* p. 32.
9. Wittgenstein, *Letters to Russell,* p. 51.

10. *Ibid.*, p. 54.
11. Fann, *Ludwig Wittgenstein,* p. 31.
12. Wittgenstein, *Letters to Russell,* p. 58.
13. Fann, *Ludwig Wittgenstein,* p. 91.
14. Dallas High, *Language, Persons, and Belief* (New York: Oxford University Press, 1967), p. 111.
15. Fann, *Ludwig Wittgenstein,* p. 68.
16. Janik and Toulmin, *Wittgenstein's Vienna,* p. 37.
17. Paul Engelmann, *Letters from Ludwig Wittgenstein, with a Memoir* (New York: Horizon, 1968), p. 49.
18. *Ibid.*, p. 5.
19. Janik and Toulmin, *Wittgenstein's Vienna,* p. 192. (Wittgenstein's italics.)
20. William James, *The Varieties of Religious Experience* (New York: Modern Library, 1902), p. 183.
21. Engelmann, *Letters from Ludwig Wittgenstein,* p. 11.
22. *Ibid.*, p. 19.
23. Wittgenstein, *Letters to Russell,* p. 91.
24. His third brother, Kurt, killed himself during the war in order to avoid being taken captive.
25. Bartley, *Wittgenstein,* p. 98.
26. Wittgenstein, *Letters to Russell,* p. 94.
27. Engelmann, *Letters from Ludwig Wittgenstein,* p. 53.
28. *Ibid.*, p. 105.
29. *Ibid.*, p. 135.
30. High, *Language, Persons, and Belief,* p. 20.
31. Donald Hudson, *Ludwig Wittgenstein, the Bearing of His Philosophy upon Religious Belief* (London: Lutterworth Press, 1968), p. 7.
32. Norman Malcolm, *Ludwig Wittgenstein: A Memoir* (New York: Oxford University Press, 1958),p. 71.
33. *Ibid.*
34. *Ibid.*, p. 100.

5. Dietrich Bonhoeffer: Witness in an Ambiguous World

1. Eberhard Bethge, Bonhoeffer's student, friend, and nephew by marriage, has done much to make Bonhoeffer's writings available and to stimulate study of his work. Bethge has edited the *Gesammelte Schriften,* 6 vols. (Munich: Kaiser Verlag, 1958–74), and provided a detailed biography, *Dietrich Bonhoeffer: Man of Vision, Man of Courage* (New York: Harper & Row, 1970). Bethge also provides a concise review of Bonhoeffer scholarship in his latest book, *Bonhoeffer: Exile and Martyr* (New York: Seabury, 1976), pp. 11-25.
2. Bethge, *Dietrich Bonhoeffer,* p. 5.
3. Sabine Leibholz-Bonhoeffer, *The Bonhoeffers: Portrait of a Family* (New York: St. Martin's Press, 1971), p. 38.
4. Paula Bonhoeffer's reaction to Walter's death often strikes readers as out of character with the woman whose resourcefulness and firmness

NOTES

made her a center of the family's stability during the Nazi period. It is only in the light of the tragic conflict of social duty and parental responsibility—helpfully suggested in conversation by Eberhard Bethge—that the authors have been able to offer a consistent interpretation of the parents' response to Walter's death and its impact on young Dietrich.

5. Dietrich Bonhoeffer, *Letters and Papers from Prison*, ed. Eberhard Bethge; the enlarged edn. Copyright © 1953, 1967, 1971 by SCM Press, Ltd. (New York: Macmillan, 1972), pp. 166-67.

6. Dietrich Bonhoeffer, *The Communion of Saints* (New York: Harper & Row, 1963).

7. Bethge, *Dietrich Bonhoeffer*, p. 14.

8. Dietrich Bonhoeffer, *True Patriotism: Letters, Lectures, and Notes, 1939–45*, ed. E. H. Robertson (New York: Harper, 1973), pp. 211-12.

9. Bethge, *Dietrich Bonhoeffer*, p. 22.

10. *Ibid.*, pp. 32-34.

11. *Ibid.*, p. 40.

12. Bonhoeffer's fascination with the idea of a visit to India persisted well into the 1930s, while his goals for the trip grew more and more specific. The initial motivation, Bethge tells us, was "a vague and general thirst for new experience." By 1934 his goal was to meet Gandhi and to learn his theory and technique of nonviolent resistance. See Bethge, *Dietrich Bonhoeffer*, pp. 74, 107, 329-32.

13. For a comprehensive study of Bonhoeffer's first American visit see Ruth Zerner, "Dietrich Bonhoeffer's American Experiences," *Union Seminary Quarterly Review* (summer, 1976), pp. 261-82.

14. Dietrich Bonhoeffer, *No Rusty Swords: Letters, Lectures and Notes, 1928–36*, ed. E. H. Robertson (New York: Harper & Row, 1965), p. 120.

15. *Ibid.*, p. 123.

16. *Ibid.*, p. 225.

17. Bethge, *Dietrich Bonhoeffer*, p. 206.

18. *No Rusty Swords*, p. 225.

19. See Bethge, *Dietrich Bonhoeffer*, pp. 24-29.

20. Dietrich Bonhoeffer, *Creation and Fall (New York: Macmillan, 1959), p. 14.*

21. *Letter to his brother-in-law Rüdiger Schleicher, April 1936. Quoted in Bethge, Dietrich Bonhoeffer, pp. 155-56.*

22. "Guiding Principles of the Faith Movement of the German Christians," Article 10 (June 6, 1932). Reprinted in A. S. Cochrane, *The Church's Confession Under Hitler* (Philadelphia: Westminster Press, 1962).

23. *Gesammelte Schriften*, II, 79.

24. Bethge, *Dietrich Bonhoeffer*, pp. 154-55.

25. Dietrich Bonhoeffer, *The Way to Freedom: Letters, Lectures and Notes 1935–39*, ed. E. H. Robertson (New York: Harper 1966), pp. 93-94.

26. See above, p. 163.

27. *The Way to Freedom* (New York: Harper & Row, 1966), p. 320.

28. *No Rusty Swords*, pp. 102-3.
29. *Ibid.*, p. 93.
30. *Letters and Papers from Prison*, pp. 369-70.
31. Dietrich Bonhoeffer, *Ethics*, ed. Eberhard Bethge (New York: Macmillan, 1955), p. 115.
32. *Ethics*, p. 343.
33. *Letters and Papers from Prison*, p. 3.
34. See page 166-67 above. See also Bethge, *Dietrich Bonhoeffer*, p. 387.
35. *Gesammelte Schriften*, I, 50.
36. "Suffering" stanza from the poem "Stations on the Road to Freedom," *Letters and Papers from Prison*, p. 371.
37. *Ibid.*, p. 279.
38. *Ibid.*, pp. 382-83.
39. "Who Am I?" *Letters and Papers from Prison*, pp. 347-48.
40. *I Knew Dietrich Bonhoeffer*, ed. Wolf-Dieter Zimmerman and Ronald Gregor Smith (New York: Harper & Row, 1966), p. 232.
41. "Death," the final stanza of "Stations on the Road to Freedom," *Letters and Papers from Prison*, p. 371.
42. *Gesammelte Schriften*, IV, 613-20. Oddly enough this poem alone among Bonhoeffer's prison poetry has not been published in English translation. The verses presented here were translated by Robin Lovin.
43. *Gesammelte Schriften*, II, 529.

Conclusion

1. Michael R. LaChat, "The Involvement of Martin Heidegger in the Nazi Party: A Faith-Developmental Analysis," Unpublished paper. Harvard University, 1975.
2. See Eberhard Bethge, *Dietrich Bonhoeffer* (New York: Harper, 1970), p. 431.
3. Alfred North Whitehead, *Religion in the Making* (New York: Meridian, 1960), p. 16.